Making and Managing an

ANTIQUE SHOP

Making and Managing an

Antique Shop

RONALD PEARSALL

David & Charles
Newton Abbot London North Pomfret (Vt)

British Library Cataloguing in Publication Data
Pearsall, Ronald
Making and managing an antique shop
1. Antique dealers – Great Britain
I. Title
658'.91'74510941 NK1110
ISBN 0–7153–8905–X

First published 1979
New revised edition 1986

Typeset by Trade Linotype Ltd., Birmingham
and printed in Great Britain
by A. Wheaton & Co. Ltd., Hennock Road, Exeter
for David & Charles Publishers plc
Brunel House Newton Abbot Devon

Published in the United States of America
by David & Charles Inc
North Pomfret Vermont 05053 USA

Contents

1 The pleasures of antique dealing

The antique trade is unique in that there is an opening in it for anyone who is interested in old things—not necessarily all old things or even antiques in their true sense (i.e. items made before 1830). One can be young or old, and spend as much or as little time on the trade as one wishes. It is one of the few businesses that can be carried on with a bare minimum of capital—even as little as £50 or £60. The range of options is endless, so much so that it is wise to spend a good deal of time thinking about one's own approach at the outset rather than rushing around buying bits and pieces on a hit-or-miss basis.

The pleasures of antique dealing far outweigh the occasional discomforts or anxieties. In the joy of the chase one can afford to overlook what in another context would be called conditions of employment. In working for oneself it is easy to tolerate standing in a draughty market on a winter morning or squelching up a farm track in pursuit of something that may or may not be desirable.

It is the element of the unexpected that makes antique dealing so genuinely exciting. Writers in antique magazines and women's papers often lament that so many antiques are exported that there are few left in this country. This is utter rubbish, written by outsiders who don't know what they are talking about. Certainly it is true that 'classic' pieces have priced themselves out of the average dealer's reach, but this is historically inevitable. It has always happened, and always will happen. Attention merely switches to something else, which has hitherto been disregarded. Nevertheless, it is still possible in the course of one's travels to come across classic pieces that are not recognised as such by their owners and that are regarded as old-fashioned and not nearly so useful as a cabinet from the nearest chain-store. In such a situation, prices are agreed on the basis of the usefulness of the object in question.

I have introduced the money angle at this stage deliberately. The aim of antique dealing is to buy something and sell it at a profit. It is as simple as that. At some stage, one will buy something intending to sell it, but will find that it is so attractive and endearing that it demands to be kept and loved. That is the test of the true dealer—to be able to turn down a sale.

Almost everyone interested in the arts and in old things must at some time or other have speculated on how pleasant it would be to run an antique business. Too often such people have been frightened off by the mystique that surrounds the trade or have been beset by hypothetical problems. For the cautious, it might be wise to ease oneself into the trade gradually; if one has a job, one could take a stall at a weekly market or antiques fair on a Sunday or during a holiday and see how it goes. At the very least, one meets interesting people; the great majority of antique dealers are decent people, especially those in the middle range. An engaging personality is worth a lot of specialized knowledge. Knowledge is by no means unimportant, but instinct is sometimes a better guide. If you like something, someone else will also like it, whether it is trendy, fashionable, unfashionable, odd, useless, or what-have-you.

2 The antique scene—past and present

An antique passes through several hands before it reaches the end of its journey, and even then it may only have arrived at a temporary halt; antiques are in constant circulation. They are bought by the general public, by companies and even by trade unions. They are treasured for one or more of the following reasons: for their beauty, or because they are useful, or because they are good investments. All antiques appreciate at a rate far higher than the rate of inflation.

Widespread trading in antiques is a fairly recent phenomenon, and until the twentieth century collectors were far more important than dealers. The great days of collecting were between 1720 and 1830, when the English gentleman could outbuy anyone and Europe was in such a state of confusion that a collector on the Grand Tour could purchase anything he set his mind to without drawing too much on his credit. He became a connoisseur, and travelled with a tame antiquary who pointed out what was worth buying and made the initial approach to the owner.

Freelance agents travelled throughout Europe, especially in Italy, and brought back antiques, selling them to the aristocracy or disposing of them at auction sales (Sotheby's opened in 1744 and Christie's in 1762). Picture dealers came later (Agnew did not start up in London until 1860). This is rather surprising, as pictures were considered to be the centre of the antique world, and furniture was not considered fit to be mentioned in the same breath. No piece of furniture was worth more than an oil painting of middling quality, and dealers in furniture were looked upon as common traders who if they entered the great Georgian houses at all, went in by the side-entrance.

Georgian collectors bought, but rarely sold; a collection remained intact until sold at auction after the death of its owner. There was little expertise except among those interested in pictures. Genuine antiques were so plentiful that there was no point in producing fakes. The rise of the industrial middle classes in the nineteenth century transformed the scene although they also bought pictures, often indiscriminately. To their eternal credit, however, they sponsored contemporary artists.

The problem for this new wealthy class was what to buy; it had immense money, but little idea of how to spend it. Manufacturers soon provided objects, and no one needs to be told of the vast range of Victoriana of all kinds. To the *nouveau riche* there was often no comparison between contemporary products and those of the previous age. Georgian furniture was considered to be flimsy-looking and bare, and was thrown out or relegated to attics or basements.

The growth of museums following the Museums Act of 1845 made an interest in general antiques respectable, and the purchase of items other than pictures brought into existence the dealer in *objets d'art* and curiosities. There was even, for the first time, an interest in old porcelain and pottery, though the first attempt at making sense of marks and monograms was not effected until 1863.

During the second half of the nineteenth century, people tended to accumulate objects rather in the manner of a magpie and we can see how overwhelming this could be in photographs of interiors of the period which show every horizontal surface loaded with bits and pieces. This delight in clutter was shared by all the moneyed classes from Queen Victoria down; it became impossible for many people to discard anything. But thanks to them today's antique dealer is able to find the stock to deck out his shop or stall.

As the working classes became more affluent they too began to buy bright new things to decorate their homes: fairings, Staffordshire figures, tea-sets, coloured prints, and the mass-produced furniture, now known as 'shipping gear'. They did not frequent curio shops, which were few in number and catered for the higher levels of society.

In the 1870s and 1880s the middle classes were not able to buy as cheaply as they had previously been able to. One of the reasons for this was the emergence of American buyers with a continent to fill with antiques from Europe and highly-paid agents to do their buying for them, agents who themselves became millionaires from the commissions they earned. Americans bought anything if it was authenticated, and there was a good deal of faking and misrepresentation. The Americans were opposed in the sale-rooms not only by the British 'shopocracy'—shopkeepers who had started in a small way and had founded chain-stores and emporiums—but by buyers for continental museums and art galleries. The trustees and backers of British museums and galleries were notorious for their reluctance to part with money, preferring to wait for some great collection to fall into their hands when a rich patriot died (such as Jones, who enriched the Victoria and Albert Museum). Such donors knew they would have galleries named after them.

The extent of the double-dealing on the part of the experts and agents who bought for the shopocracy and the Americans was often not discovered until the buyers had died and their collections were dispersed at auction. But towards the end of the nineteenth century a good deal more knowledge was made available to those who were interested in antiques, and a number of art magazines appeared with articles by experts who had really done their homework. The bargain hunters appeared, buying objects not for their intrinsic value but for their profit potential.

With the death of Queen Victoria, there was a revulsion against the opulence and obsessive detail that had characterized many of the products of her age. The Edwardian smashing of Victoriana can be compared with the burning of books by the Nazis in the 1930s. Genuine antiques were still plentiful, but the antique dealer remained a lowly creature. Although mahogany was back in favour after the years of fumed oak, walnut, and rosewood, the Edwardians preferred their reproduction Georgian to the real thing. Only a few antique dealers, who dealt in fine French furniture and renaissance treasures, were in the first flight. The general dealer was a rather grubby sort of person akin to a pawnbroker, who sold second-hand objects to people who could not afford something new.

The various trends between the wars kept the dealers on their toes. *Art nouveau* flickered out in the 1920s, and the simple designs of the functional movement made everything else appear *passé*; Art Deco bits and pieces, suitably modified for the lower-middle classes, replaced time-honoured ornaments, some of them of considerable merit. These found their way to the junk man and perhaps the general dealer, where they languished. There was no public interest in antiques. A few discerning collectors made polite forays into the more curious and baroque manifestations of Victoriana. These objects were considered interesting analogues to Surrealist artefacts.

The people who were below the Art Deco appreciation line or who were poor retained furniture and bric-à-brac handed down from generation to generation. There was no realization of what these objects were, from what period they came, or if they had any value. They had always been about the place, and always would be, passing in time to their owner's children. Little as they knew it at the time, these people were guardians of part of our heritage.

Social mobility was greatly accelerated by World War II and those effected by it became aware of the way in which other people lived and were introduced to a life style and an environment previously unknown to them. The affluence of the 1950s and 1960s made the general public acquisitive, and when the media began to exploit antiques there was no class barrier to break down. As far as the general public was concerned, the big breakthrough came with television, with the more spectacular sales at Sotheby's and Christie's covered in newsreels and current affairs programmes. The items in such sales were no doubt greeted by the audience with oohs and aahs, but a vase is a vase and a picture is a picture and no matter how ludicrous the comparisons television viewers looked around their sitting-rooms and began to make valuations of their own antiques. More significant still was the success of the television programme *Going for a Song* which often dealt with quite humble objects of the kind owned by ordinary people. The most important thing was not the age or beauty of the objects under scrutiny by Arthur Negus and his guests but the price they put on it.

To cater for the great public interest in antiques and a new category called collectables a number of new magazines appeared. Most of them have gone, but some have prospered and are still with us, deserving their success. Popular newspapers began to run an antiques column, and antiques or mock-antiques began to be appreciated as status symbols that, unlike the prime status symbol the car, could be turned into ready cash at short notice—and make a profit.

For the first time ordinary people were looking for antiques, and the old regiment of long-established antique dealers were joined by amateurs and semi-professionals who opened shops and manned stalls to cater for the growing demand. Running an antique shop was a thoroughly respectable occupation; indeed, there was a kind of kudos about it, and actresses who were 'resting' and minor public figures found that this type of shopkeeping made them rather more interesting than they had been before.

Anything could be collected and, if the portents were right, anything could be construed as an antique. This boom time coincided with European affluence, and big dealers became bigger by exporting antiques, especially furniture, to the Continent in massive quantities. The available goods were dispersed among more and more dealers, and new categories of antiques were found and exploited, each to find an expert or pseudo-expert to pontificate on it in the press. Price-guides arrived on the scene to help systematize values—a retrograde step in the opinion of the trade.

Recession cut down the numbers of amateurs and part-timers. There was little surplus cash about, and although dealers in high-class antiques did not suffer overmuch, those in the medium and lower ranges soon had their backs to the wall. They were not helped by the sudden increase in property prices that made it difficult to start shops, and the even more frightening increase in rates that made an existing shop a more expensive place to keep going. A dealer who had previously just made ends meet could no longer do so. Junk-dealers were the most vulnerable; they operated on low profit margins and low overheads, and could no longer survive.

This unhappy period for the trade is now in the past, and stability has returned. Foreign buyers, both private and trade, are active and the dramatic increase in antiques markets and fairs provide outlets for newcomers to the trade.

The most important development is the increasing importance of auction rooms, which use modern publicity methods to make themselves known to the public. Many of the larger auction houses now provide an 'advisory service'; members of the firms travel around the country and set up in a hotel or hall and make valuations of goods people bring to them, hopefully to entice the owners to sell the items through their auction room.

This, naturally, is of no help to the antique trade, but dealers expect this enthusiasm for giving advice to founder eventually. The trade has had its problems before, and overcome them.

3 Where to sell—the shop . . .

There are three questions the prospective antique dealer has to ask himself or herself. The first is: how much buying capital have I got? The second and third questions depend for their answers on the answer to question one. The second is: which is the best way, bearing in mind the money I have available, to carry on the business? The third is: should I buy anything, or should I specialize?

Antique dealing can be carried out on many different levels. The most obvious way is from a shop, but this means having the money to buy or rent one. A shop is by no means essential, indeed, many successful dealers with ample funds prefer not to have one. They have stalls at antique fairs and antique markets, and find that this is sufficient. Newcomers to antiques often enter at the lowest level by taking a stall at a weekly market, alongside stalls selling fruit and veg, cast-off clothing, paperbacks, and plastic gnomes. One can sell from one's own house, which is a method not to be ignored—if one doesn't mind strangers stomping through the sitting-room and making offers for everything that takes their fancy.

Some dealers have no shop, no stall, nor indeed any permanent or semi-permanent outlet—with the exception of their cars. They are known as 'runners' and deal from the boots of their cars or, more often, from the backs of their vans. It is only fair to say that the trade treats them with a good deal of suspicion. 'Runners' often deal purely with 'shippers' (big dealers who do not open their warehouses to the general public and who are solely concerned with the overseas market, exporting antiques in containers).

Why are runners regarded with suspicion? The answer is that by and large antique dealers are law-abiding citizens, and runners are often fly-by-nights, anonymous creatures who might easily be trying to sell 'bent gear' (stolen goods). The police, rightly, are very hot on dealers dishonestly handling stolen property ('dishonestly handling' was formerly known as 'receiving'), and most dealers would rather forego a good purchase than risk buying suspect antiques. In some areas, especially in the provinces, the police issue lists of stolen property, but the crime rate is now so high that in large towns and cities the compilation of such lists is not possible.

If one is considering opening a shop there are a number of factors to take into account. In the first place, where should it be? Town or city, or in the country? For those who wish to escape the rat-race, and perhaps have already got a successful career behind them, the lure of the country village is difficult to resist. To those accustomed to inflated property prices in the city, substantial village properties can seem very reasonably priced, but there is no point in opening an antique shop to which no one comes. There are villages and villages. Some have a built-in tourist appeal, and might therefore, appear to be ideal locations, but the question must be asked: what kind of tourists do these villages attract?

The English holidaymaker is not a buyer of antiques, especially when towing a caravan and stocking up at the local supermarket. Motorways have brought into rural areas urban dwellers who would not be seen dead with an antique in their homes, and it would be idle to pretend that they are going to provide custom for the antique dealer. Foreign tourists are a different matter. In Germany especially, young couples are delighted to furnish their homes with antiques as it enhances their status. Conventional beauty spots and pretty-pretty villages attract the home-grown holidaymaker like a bee to nectar, but foreigners are more inclined to head for historically interesting towns and villages, such as Chichester, Totnes, or Winchester. So if you are intent on catering for the foreign tourist or the more intellectually-inclined British one you must take this into consideration when deciding on a location for your shop.

If the final choice is a shop in a city, the outer suburbs should be avoided like the plague. Except in prestige suburbs such as Surbiton or Wimbledon, local custom cannot sustain an antique shop, and, more to the point, the trade will not come, except by accident. The trade sustains the trade, and newcomers to antique dealing will be astonished when they find out how much business is done between dealers. At times, he or she will genuinely begin to feel that there is no such thing as a private buyer—though, logically, that is where the antique eventually ends up.

Inner city areas are a different matter, and many run-down neighbourhoods have been given new life by the emergence of a crop of antique shops. This happens especially in areas due for redevelopment. The shops in such areas are on a short lease, and the general air of seediness often encourages the trade to believe that here there are bargains to be had. As indeed there often are. Overheads and rates are low, and profit margins can be cut to give the buyer the extra pound or two that makes the difference between a buyer and a browser.

However, buying a property often depends on chance rather than choice, and no situation—except the outer suburb—is a loss if the contents of the antique shop are interesting and of the type that people will buy, even if the shop is set in a village of no great consequence in an area of no natural beauty whatsoever. It helps if the shop can be seen from a main road; no antique dealer will pass a shop that seems worth a visit. It is even better if there is more than one shop to go to, even if the village population numbers a mere two hundred.

M.M.A.B.—B

It is often the case that where an antique shop opens in a village or small town, others will follow. The reason is not that the village is particularly well placed, but that a number of shops will make it worthwhile for a dealer to make a detour of perhaps twenty miles from a motorway or arterial road to call. That is the theory, but some antique dealers resent the influx of other shops, not because they are unsociable but because it reduces the chance of a 'call-out'.

The call-out is, to be frank, one of the main reasons for opening a shop. A call-out occurs when a private person goes into a shop with something to sell, or offers the shopkeeper the chance to buy 'gear' from his or her house. There are still treasures to be found in the most unlikely surroundings, and this is where the thrill of the chase comes in. In such a situation the dealer has to make an on-the-spot assessment of articles which may be unfamiliar to him and with which—to make no bones about it—he may well feel all at sea. No dealer can be expected to know everything, and at call-outs, the most stimulating part of the trade, it is necessary to trust one's instinct, giving a realistic price yet having a gamble at the same time. On the other hand, it should be said that it is very easy to come fearfully unstuck on such occasions and to pay unrealistic prices for objects not far removed from junk. The private person can often be astonishingly shrewd and well-primed from hours spent watching *Going for a Song.*

There is thus a strong case for settling on a village or small town with no existing antique shop, for by buying well from the locals it is possible to sell well, leaving a margin for someone else to make a profit also. It must be constantly emphasized that antiques can change hands seven or eight times before they reach their ultimate destination, and that there is a strong incentive to be first in the line. Buying well does not mean being unscrupulous. It is often best to pay above the market price for being mean brings its own retribution if only because the word gets round and the hoped-for supply of goods is not forthcoming.

If a suitable shop has been found, it is wise to make a few preliminary inquiries about the place. Has there, for instance, been an antique shop in the village before, and if so why did it close? What kind of shopping facilities already exist for tourists and the passing trade? A good quality crafts shop is a plus, and so is a second-hand bookshop. A plethora of cheap gift shops selling miniature potties and plaster ducks are a definite minus as this sort of shop springs up in direct answer to demand. Are there flourishing antique shops in the nearest big town or city? If so, this is an advantage, as the newcomer has potential customers on the door-step.

If there are already antique shops in the village it is a good idea to pay them a visit, keeping your motives hidden as yet. You will have to use your powers of observation and your instinct to ascertain whether they are doing well or badly. A lot of dust on the items for sale is a bad sign, as are dog-eared price tags; even more revealing are price tags where the price has been dropped, a sure sign of desperation. A polite inquiry, 'How's business?' is in order, but any answer must be taken with a pinch of salt. If you look like a possible 'punter' (buyer) the dealer will certainly not tell you that business is bad.

Parking facilities are very important. Dealers on the road are not very keen on too much walking, and double yellow lines outside the shop and a car park a quarter of a mile away is not a promising start. A single yellow line is all right. An antique dealer parking his car on a single yellow line outside a shop is always 'loading' (allowed by law) whether it is true or not. No lines at all is obviously best. It is also good to be in a stretch of straight road with unhampered visibility, so that a passing motorist can register the existence of an antique shop and have plenty of time to draw up to the kerb.

In making inquiries about the shop, it is very important to ask the owner or estate agent if there are any odd restrictions about usage. Normally, there are not. Antique shops are regarded as an asset and an amenity, but the question of a change of usage should be thoroughly looked into.

The aspiring dealer will know whether he wants to live on the premises, and will evaluate the living accommodation according to his requirements. It is advantageous to live on the premises, if only to catch trade buyers who may pass through at odd times; it is also an asset when it comes to taking out insurance against fire, damage, or burglary. The premises should be inspected with an eye to their potential; a coat of paint can transform a scruffy depressing shop. A double window is an asset; it is the point of sale, and an interesting display can bring in waverers.

There are two schools of thought regarding lighting, but by and large dim atmospheric lighting is not to be recommended, except in very high-class establishments where a piece of silver priced at £1000 has every right to regal treatment. Some dealers of the old school retain their 15-watt bulbs in the hope that a customer will buy pottery with a minute chip in it or furniture that is not quite what it seems to be (perhaps a 'marriage', an item made up of two or more cannibalized pieces). Well-placed fluorescent lighting is as good as any, though there is a lot to be said for natural light, if it is available, especially if paintings and jewellery are to be sold.

It is important to have good shelving, and if there is shelving already in place it can save several hundred pounds at the current price of wood. The condition of the walls should be examined, with a view to knocking hooks in them for the display of pictures, but this is perhaps of minor importance in view of the adaptibility of Rawlplugs, and the availability of peg-board.

Store-rooms are a great asset. There will always be items waiting to be collected or waiting to be repaired, and big pieces of furniture in a shop can dwarf everything else. Store-rooms are also useful in that they can house additional items so that the shop stock can be switched around to avoid staleness. The surest way to sell something that happens to be sticking is to put it somewhere else, or waft it out of sight for a week. And, a psychological point, other antique dealers are always more inclined to buy from a hidden source. 'Anything in the back?' they will ask, and if there is, so much the better.

If there is access to the store-room other than through the shop, this is a decided advantage. The transport of large pieces of furniture through a crowded antique shop can be a nerve-racking experience.

There is a choice between buying or renting a shop. Renting can be on a monthly basis, especially in villages or country towns where there is little competition for shop premises. But, as with purchasing a leasehold property, one has to watch for the hidden extras. In leasehold properties rent reviews are the order of the day, usually carried out at five-yearly intervals. There may also be massive rate increases, which can cripple a business whether it be freehold or leasehold.

The advantage of renting a shop rather than buying is that it releases capital for buying antiques. It is foolish to sink one's all in a shop and have no money left with which to buy stock. This is a matter of common sense, but in venturing into unknown territory, common sense can sometimes be buried under enthusiasm.

A mere ten years ago, a shop was the natural outlet for the antique dealer, but the whole emphasis of the trade has shifted since then. Today a shop is only one of the many options open to a dealer. The advantages of a shop are clear. It is both an outlet and a buying point. The stock is there, and does not have to be shifted around; it can be displayed to its best effect.

But a shop does have its disadvantages.

First, a shop is a tie. It has to be opened at a certain time and closed at a certain time. This leaves less time for buying, travelling, and visiting auctions. There is much to be said for a husband and wife team or two friends in partnership, where one can do the buying and the other can do the selling. There are times when running a shop can be deadly boring. Unlike a tobacconist's or a bakery, there is unlikely to be a constant volume of customers in an antique shop, and the proportion of browsers rather than buyers can often seem excessive. Except in well-favoured spots, the months from January to April can seem very long—few people about and even fewer buying. During these months the trade goes into hibernation, and many dealers close their shops for the whole of the period, the luckier of them wintering in Spain or elsewhere. (This may happen to you!)

The viability of an antique business does not depend on volume of trade. This is especially true of specialist dealers; one specialist dealer in Brighton rarely has more than half a dozen customers a week. But there is little on sale for less than £600 or £700. This particular dealer is fortunate not only in his choice of specialist subject, but in the fact that his antiques are usually big and bulky. He is not troubled by the international pastime that provides a minor reason for not taking a shop—theft, and in particular shoplifting.

Until the mid-1960s an antique dealer could sit with his feet up in his cubby-hole, den, or sitting-room (depending on his preference) until a potential customer rang a little bell, or called out, or made his presence known in some other way. At this point the dealer would drag himself (or herself) to his feet and find out what it was all about. A browser or a time-waster would not infringe on the dealer's time; he or she would potter around and go. Alas, times have changed. It is a sad state of affairs, but no longer can the casual customer be left to browse, because the stranger in the shop may be a thief. The odds are higher if the person is a foreign student, many of whom regard property as a personal affront, higher still if the students drift in in threes and fours and betray an extraordinary interest in silver and jewellery, which is easy to pocket and equally easy to dispose of. No antique dealer should leave small silver and jewellery within reach of an idle hand; such items should be in a locked cabinet that is opened only on request.

To protect his own interests, a dealer is now obliged to hang around the shop while customers peruse the stock, just to watch out for the 2 or 3 per cent of wrong 'uns. One has to be philosophical about it. Honesty is on the down grade, and even with the beadiest eyes in the world, a dealer must expect to lose one or two items to shoplifters. The only hope is that the shoplifter is as ignorant as he is dishonest, and carries away some fairly unimportant object.

This leads to one of the objections to employing help in the shop. A paid employee cannot be expected to be as vigilant as the owner, and it is not unusual for a dear old thing who is willing to sit in while the owner goes to an auction to be intimidated by a thief or thieves, though the customary procedure is for a team to go in, one engaging the shopkeeper in conversation while the others slip things into pockets or, more often, into cavernous shopping-bags.

What is the law doing? one may indignantly ask. The law does what it can, but a shoplifter is out of the shop and mingling with the crowd before the police arrive. And if a shoplifter is caught, what happens? A small fine, if that. If a foreign student is caught the odds are that he or she will get a talking to from the police, and be despatched back to his or her country of origin. In some seaside resorts, which are easily reached by day-trippers from the Continent, special magistrates' courts are set up just to deal with foreign shoplifters.

All in all, shoplifting is a minor irritation for the antique dealer; it is never a major problem as it is for the London department stores or for supermarkets. But it is wise to realize that there are more dishonest people about than there once were, and to take precautions accordingly—small and expensive items in locked cabinets, a loud trusty bell on the door if the owner lives on the premises and is not always in the shop, and no big lumps of furniture blocking the view.

Shoplifted goods are goods lost; goods burgled can be covered by insurance (but read the small print—there is usually a proviso excluding 'real' jewellery).

The photographs between pages 25–30 and 65–68 illustrate a typical provincial antiques fair. At this weekly fair in Newton Abbot there are more than forty stalls and it has become a most successful event, attracting trade buyers, collectors and members of the public.

For the beginner, a stall at one of the many casual fairs is a very good introduction to the trade. The organizer will usually be on hand to give advice, otherwise consult *Art & Antiques Weekly* which publishes notices about forthcoming fairs.

Stalls at permanent antique fairs are normally let on an annual basis. Many casual fairs, lasting one, two or three days, are held all over the country. The price of a stall at a London fair will be rather more expensive.

(photographs by Jerome Dessain)

4 . . . Or the stall

It is no longer infra dig to be a shopkeeper; the boutique explosion in the 1960s made it trendy. It is not many years since a person who stood at a stall was regarded as nothing but a glorified rag-and-bone merchant. Now, however, there is nothing socially reprehensible in being a stall-holder, whether it is in a prestigious antique supermarket such as Antiquarius in the King's Road, Chelsea, or in an open market in the provinces.

Portobello Road and Bermondsey Market made antique stall-holding respectable: professionals and amateurs took it up. Dealers supplemented the earnings of their shops, actors and actresses earned a bit of pin money when they were 'resting', aspirants to the business who happened to have a Saturday morning spare saw a way of making money and having an amusing time as well.

Antique supermarkets represent a compromise between the stall and the shop. The stalls are really mini-shops, with continuity of occupation and the climatic hazards of open stalls blissfully forgotten. The market's management usually supplies lighting facilities, sometimes meshes for security, and can often arrange for stalls to be 'covered' when the renters are away, i.e., someone sells for the occupant.

One of the major drawbacks of the antique supermarket is that space is usually limited. Often the stall is a mere 36 sq ft. An advantage, however, is that a collection of perhaps a hundred dealers gathered in one place encourages other dealers to call and buy. The idea was good, and many antique supermarkets have gone on to flourish, but disillusionment has crept in, and the excitement has gone out of the supermarket. The fact that the supermarket is open six days a week robs it of impact. Visiting dealers often feel that the goods are jaded, that they have been going the rounds from dealer to dealer, and that anything that is really interesting has been whisked away out of circulation by an earlier bargain-spotter. The sort of antique indigestion that one can get from a stroll down Portobello Road on a Saturday morning is much worse in a claustrophobic indoor market, where the goods on one stall seem to be almost interchangeable with those on the one next to it, with matching prices and matching dust. If one is a specialist, one feels that other specialists have been through the stuff already. Antique supermarkets are good for hitherto disregarded items that have yet to become collectable, and those on fashionable sites (such as the one behind Selfridge's in Oxford Street and the Antique Hypermarket in Kensington) attract the private buyer.

Several antique supermarkets went out of business within a year or two, so it is clear that they were not all they were expected to be, and the massive influx of trade did not materialize. The real buyers did not turn up, preferring to shop at the traditional outlets, Bermondsey Market on Friday morning, Portobello Road and Camden Passage on Saturday.

In the 1960s, Bermondsey Market (also known as the Caledonian Market because it was once on the site of the Caledonian Meat Market in north London) was the primary trade market. Business started at 3 or 4 am on Friday morning. It was then principally an open market, officially run, with stall-holders keeping their places year after year, son succeeding father on the same pitch of ground. There was no chance of newcomers getting a stall; the only way to sell there was to come to some sharing arrangement with an existing stall-holder. Most of the stall-holders turned up at a civilized hour (8 am or so), and until then it was an illegal free-for-all, with lorries and vans packed to overflowing creeping in and antiques being sold from the backs of the lorries or from the pavements.

East-End junk men and women set up on the roadside selling from their suitcases. Sometimes a suitcase could contain several thousand pounds worth of silver. The dealers were not there for pennies.

It was a gutsy, exciting market, but recently the steam has gone out of it. Surrounding warehouses have been turned into indoor markets, and the immediacy associated with outdoor buying and selling has been lost. Trade starts on Thursday afternoon, and the market has lost its 'trade only' feel. Formerly, it was a prelude to the big day at Portobello Road, but now they are little different from each other with tourists and rubber-neckers finding it a good way to spend an hour or two.

The open market area is still the centre of Bermondsey trade, and it is still virtually impossible to get a stall there. For those who fancy being at the centre of things, it is worth enquiring whether there are indoor stalls available, but Bermondsey has lost its status as the one important trade market. There is still an antiques and bric-à-brac area in Petticoat Lane on Sunday morning, but like Bermondsey the Petticoat Lane market has lost its status.

Partly this is because antique markets have opened in London in the most diverse of places, as well as in the provinces, but it is also a result of the arrival of the antiques fair. At this stage one may ask 'What is the difference between a fair and a market?' The answer is: often very little. The antique fair is a fairly new arrival to this country though well known on the Continent, where there has never been a large number of antique shops such as Britain has possessed since World War II. The fairs are up-graded markets, and those who run them prefer to see antiques on the stalls rather than rubbish, frowning on reproduction brass and copper and sometimes setting a 'date-line'. For example, in the prospectus, the organizer may specify that items later than 1900 are not allowed, and reserve the right to ask stall-holders to remove such items from their stalls. The highest level of antique fair insists on 'true' antiques; this excludes Victoriana and everything later than the

1830s. Naturally this fair excludes most of the middle-range antique dealers.

Many fair organizers, however, even if they specify a date-line, add a proviso; 'collectors' items' are allowed. And collectors' items can be anything. The main aim of fair organizers is not to be awkward, but to keep out junk dealers, so a newcomer to the antique trade need not be alarmed by what might seem to be fussy restrictions. At its most blunt, fair organizers want the kind of dealers who fit in.

Antique fairs can be one-day, two-day, or three-day events. They can be held in a variety of venues—town halls, assembly halls, country clubs, or hotels—especially large hotels which have a conference room or a ballroom. The number of stalls can vary from forty upwards and the organizers often supply tables and lighting. For one-day fairs, opening hours vary, with 10 am being the most usual. Closing times can be from 3 pm to 7 pm. For two- and three-day fairs, the hours are staggered, with usually one late-night opening. Stall charges for one-day fairs vary from £12 to £20 a day, more for the *true* antiques fairs, and the general public is often charged a small admission fee. Charges for two- and three-day fairs are pro rata.

Fairs can be great fun, and at regular venues they can be almost like reunions. There is no better way for a newcomer to antiques to start than to have a stall at an antiques fair; one gets to know people and, it is worth remembering, one can obtain genuine free advice from one's more experienced colleagues. There is no trace of the cut-throat competition that can make auctions rather tiresome.

How does one find out where fairs are being held and to whom does one apply? Dozens of fairs are held each week in Britain, they take place on various days, and are advertised in *Antiques Trade Gazette*. Almost always, they are exceptionally well run by someone in antiques, and it is usual for an organizer to arrange a sequence of fairs within easy driving distance of each other. If one takes part in one fair and it is satisfactory, one is inclined to book up for the later ones.

The fair's popularity has greatly extended the buying and selling capacity of the ordinary dealer, and there is no question that the fair is here to stay, probably pushing the shop outlet into second place in terms of importance and turnover. A parallel can be seen in the High Street, where the supermarket and chain store have squeezed the small shopkeeper almost to extinction.

In terms of the kind of goods offered for sale, many antique markets are akin to fairs. The main distinction is that markets are held usually weekly and always at the same place, so giving continuity. The charge for a stall at a market is about £8-£10. Some of them (as with London's antique supermarkets) are divided up into cubicles, and goods can be left from one week to the next. At some of them, tables are provided, while at others sellers bring their own trestle tables (the most useful kind being wallpaper-pasting tables, which fold in two, are light, and take up little space in the car, fitting comfortably between the front and back seats).

There is a greater range of goods at markets, even so-called antique markets, and the odd junk dealer manages to infiltrate them, as well as the purveyor of cheap jewellery (bought from Birmingham and sold at double the original price). Of course, as in the London supermarkets, there are 'markets' that remain open all week, but these are not true markets in the traditional sense of the word. The one-day market is the best in every way, both for buying and selling, because the stock is new (or, at least, appears new—shifting the stock around from week to week makes a stall look entirely different).

The antique markets are all of a piece. There is less difference between an antique fair and an antique market than between the antique market and the street market, in which antique and bric-à-brac stalls rub against fruit and vegetable stalls and those selling cast-off clothing. Bric-à-brac technically means old curiosities, knick-knacks 'or other treasured odds and ends'. In the vernacular it means a crazy medley, and a dealer at a street market can sell everything, from the lower-grade antiques such as swing-mirrors, copper kettles, and pretty plates, to old enamel bowls and plastic beads. These open-air markets usually take place on the town's market day, and they are essentially a rural phenomenon. Usually they are run by the local council with an inspector of markets to lay down the rules, allocate places, and see that no one oversteps the allotted space. The charges for stall-holders are very low, a pound or two at most, but at the most popular street markets there is a waiting list for places.

In recent years, people with an open space at their disposal (such as pub managers) have turned such areas as car-parks into weekly open markets. Some have survived, but the majority have not, especially if they are in out-of-the-way towns and villages and, as is customary, there is little or no advertising. A fairly new phenomenon is the boot fair where *anything* is sold from the boots of cars. These are advertised in local papers, the usual charge for sellers being £3 a car, while buyers are admitted to the site free.

There is nothing to stop a newcomer to the trade trying his hand at these ephemeral markets, if one happens to spring up within a few miles, but nothing sensational can ever be expected from it. If one wants to get rid of a mound of unwanted china or other domestic items these hit-and-run markets serve a purpose of a kind. At these informal affairs, charges depend on how much the owner of the land can screw out of the stall-holder. A pound would be about par for the course.

It might appear that fairs and markets (antique or street), are the answer to a dream. Why, one might ask, does *anyone* bother with a shop? There are several answers to this question. Firstly, there is very little chance of buying from private persons at a market or fair. True, people do occasionally bring in things to sell, but with thirty or forty stall-holders looking for good buys the odds are heavily against any one person being the one approached. Secondly, there is the problem of transporting the goods. Most stall-holders take small things to fairs and markets, but furniture-dealers—and furniture is the backbone of the antique trade—are obliged to weigh the changes of possible sales against the sheer nuisance of getting furniture to a venue. Furniture can be very heavy; it can also be awkward. A table with four delicate legs, a china cabinet, or a Victorian whatnot, can be very vulnerable. Not surprisingly, furniture-dealers are more in evidence at three-day fairs than at those that last only one day; at least, they do not have to bring the furniture and take it back on the same day.

Furniture also takes up a lot of room, and as the standard size of a stall at a fair is 9ft it is necessary to rent two or three spaces to accommodate even a modest amount of furniture. It then becomes a matter of weighing up rental charges against possible profit. A shop is all but essential to a dealer who seriously wants to get into furniture.

Transporting smaller items is an irritant rather than a problem. There is always a danger of breaking something, and packing and unpacking can take a considerable time. Boxes of china, copper, brass, and glass, have to be carried from the car or van to the stall, and back again when the market has closed (unless one has sold the lot). At fairs or markets it is wise to enquire whether one can park immediately outside to load or unload. One usually can, but at one-day markets held in church halls in a town or city centre one can be unpleasantly surprised and have to struggle up flights of granite steps clutching one's goods.

A dealer has to be reasonably fit to do fairs and markets. Fetching and carrying may not be to the taste of a man in his sixties who has retired and wants to start a new career in antiques. Many do it, but it is tiring for a person who has led a sedentary life.

The question of fitness also arises when it comes to considering the pros and cons of open markets. An open-air market on a beautiful summer day can be delightful, but in the winter, when the rain sweeps down and the wind strikes chill, it is a different matter. The long-standing street markets carry on throughout the year, despite the drop in custom. If a stall-holder drops out during the foul weather, he has lost his place and the chance to make money during spring, summer, and autumn.

Veteran open marketeers provide themselves with a canopy, usually of polyurethane, on a metal frame, but even with this protection a morning spent on a market in the depths of winter can be depressing. With the most efficient canopy available, there is always some way the goods on offer become wet. This may be all right for fruit and veg; but not for antiques, whether they are high or low class. Bookdealers come off worst; a brisk downpour can cut the value of their stock by half in a few minutes.

Notwithstanding the various inconveniences of the open market many stall-holders have no wish to 'up-grade' themselves. They buy their goods cheaply, and sell them cheaply, with a margin sufficient to make it worth their while. They are primary suppliers to the trade, and the dealers a rung or two above them will be buzzing around their stalls at 7 am while they unpack, and they will buy, without the ifs and maybes that characterize many private buyers. It is possible for a stall-holder at an open market to take a good deal of money in a very short time—often considerably more than an apparently more affluent dealer with a shop. Proof of this can be seen in the registration plates of the cars they unload from.

Open markets are not advertised. They are just there. The way to find out what the form is and whether there are stalls available, is to get into conversation with one of the stall-holders (buying one or two things helps). A good weekly market *can* be difficult to get into, but not always. And there are so many of them about that if one does not mind covering about twenty miles there should be one with vacancies. The open market is a good starting point for someone with as yet little confidence and a few low value items to sell. It is worth going merely to get the feel of it, and perhaps to speculate £20 or so on other stall-holders' goods. Even if one does not quite know what one is doing, pretty unbroken things in the under-£5 range can always have 50 per cent put on the buying price and be displayed for the private 'punter'.

5 Buying

The question of specialization is tied up with the availability of capital and the availability of the kind of thing one wants to deal in. It would be idiotic for a man with £200 to specialize in Bow china or fine furniture. With that sort of money he might just be able to buy a set of chairs. On the other hand, 'collectables' rather than true antiques can be bought with a very limited supply of capital, and the 'magpie' mind can make a collectable out of almost anything. Collectables might be defined as things having little or no intrinsic value, which are desirable for no other reason than that they are collected. The postage stamp is the classic example; the accumulation of stamps must have seemed an odd pursuit in the 1840s and 1850s when philately was born. There are still similar categories open for aspirant dealers. In September 1978 more than £200 was paid at auction for a small collection of advertising leaflets. The auctioneer's estimate was less than £50. Postcards, almost completely disregarded until the early 1960s, have now attained classic status.

If one is fascinated by some particular subject it would be foolish not to capitalize on this interest in the course of business. However, there is a wealth of difference between, for example, an interest in Roman coins and dealing in them. Nevertheless many people have got into antiques as a result of being a collector. As their tastes and knowledge improved, so they weeded out and sold inferior examples from their collections. Antique values have appreciated more than most, and many collectors were delighted at the prices, thus being encouraged to buy and sell for a living.

If one has decided to specialize in something, it is important to examine critically the items selected. Enthusiasts have a strange way of becoming obsessed with their subject, thinking that what seems to them of overpowering interest must be fascinating to others. This is not always so, though at times there seems no end to human perversity.

It is tempting to think of dealing in objects which seem very underpriced, objects slightly outside the antique mainstream but certainly having antique qualities. Old sewing machines, for example. These simply do not sell, even though they are in the £5 to £10 bracket. If they are bought, they are bought for use. Smaller antiques that seem to be underpriced are silver-handled button-hooks and glove-stretchers. At under £5, they seem to be worth getting hold of. But they can sit in a shop for a long time before being sold at 50p profit. The reason is that they are so boring. The same is true of pottery jelly moulds. They seem an ideal thing to collect, and as they are in the £3–£8 range they are decidedly inexpensive. People do collect them until it dawns on them that one jelly mould is very much like another, and the collections go on the rounds again.

Buying things because they are cheap is always a danger. Everyone does it, including experienced dealers. It does not necessarily mean that the item is under-priced; it may mean that no one wants it, and that it has, therefore, found its own level.

There are two ways of buying antiques—rationally, and intuitively. The rational approach means looking around and seeing something which one recognizes as being a characteristic item of its type, of a specific age, which one has seen for sale elsewhere at £*x* and which has made £*y* at auction. This presupposes knowledge of the object in question—one has done one's homework. The intuitive approach means spotting something that appeals, because it is pretty, interesting, or unusual. 'If I like it, someone else will. I have proved it before, and there is no reason to suppose that I have lost my instinct.' Women dealers favour this attitude.

But most buying necessitates taking a chance, except with cast-iron certainties, the 'standards'. A list of standards would fill a book. They comprise all the recognized antiques, and almost anything prior to 1840. One gets to know them as one acquires experience.

Where does one buy?

At auctions and house sales, from other dealers, and privately. Before a newcomer to antiques buys at auction it is advisable to visit a few sales and diligently jot down the prices obtained. It is absolutely essential to view the sale beforehand, and try to look at everything. A surprisingly low price for some lot might not mean that no one recognizes its value, but that it is damaged. A damaged item is usually marked AF ('as found') in the auctioneer's catalogue but the standard of some repair work is so high that the auctioneer's examination when cataloguing may have missed it.

Auction houses vary enormously, and it is a good idea to sample a few of them, including those which sell everything from vacuum cleaners upwards. If there are antiques in a sale otherwise devoted to rubbish, one should not assume that no one else will have spotted their existence. Runners spend half their time visiting auctions, and if there is anything worthwhile it will almost certainly be known.

Small-scale auctions often start at 2 pm, with viewing in the morning, but most auctions can be viewed on the previous day. This makes it possible for a bit of research to be done on any particularly interesting pieces the night before the sale. The bibles of the antique trade are *Lyle's Price Guide* and *Miller's Price Guide* though one has to take some of the prices given with a pinch of salt. Many of the prices set out have been taken from those obtained at auction, and there is no way of finding out whether they are reasonable or freakish—freakish due to the presence of a dealers' ring (when auction prices will be low) or to the presence of a private customer determined to outbid everybody (when prices will be high). Most of the old-established dealers wish that price guides had never been thought of, but they are here to stay, and do give a rough indication of what to expect.

When one is viewing with the intention of bidding the following day, it is vital to mark the catalogue with the top price one is prepared to pay for specific lots, and to keep to it, ignoring the competition. There may be someone in the room prepared to outbid everybody. The top amount should be an odd figure, £55 instead of the round £50 (remember that for expensive items the bidding goes up in £5 jumps, or more). If one has a pet auction room, it is a good idea to become friendly with the porter. If one is nervous, one can leave bids with him, and porters will often reveal the reserves that have been put on certain lots.

At some auctions, the buyer can 'clear' immediately, paying the clerk who will receipt the slip on which the lots have been set down. The slip is then shown to a porter, who will permit the buyer to take the goods away. If lots cannot be cleared until the auction is over, keep an eye on what you have bought, to see that no one inadvertently breaks it or drops it. Boxes of bits, in which there might be one or two nice things amongst the dross, should be watched carefully. There are unscrupulous characters at auctions who will 'lift' choice items from the box one has bought and poke them amongst their acquisitions. If on viewing day a lot has been marked in one's catalogue for possible purchase, one should always examine it on sale day, both to confirm one's wish to buy it, and to ascertain that it has come to no harm in the meantime.

An occasional buyer at auctions does not have much chance of rubbing up against the dealers' ring. The ring is there at all important auctions, but the newcomer will not know of it, unless the actions of the dealers composing the ring make it patently obvious. There is nothing particularly sinister about the ring. It is merely a group of dealers who try to buy things cheaply; they then auction the items among themselves. The only person who suffers is the vendor, who can prevent goods being sold too cheaply by putting sensible reserves on them. And, of course, the auctioneer, who loses commission.

The dealers' ring is illegal, but there has never been, nor will there ever be, a way to put a stop to it. Two hundred years ago dealers' rings operated at auctions. The argument then was the same as today: dealers are in business together; why should they cost each other money and put the cash into the hands of the person who placed the item in the sale-room? In any event, calling the ring illegal can be seen as splitting hairs. It is perfectly lawful to go 'halves' in anything—two people buying something between them; but it is unlawful if there are three or more people doing the same thing.

The law governing auction etiquette is set down in the Auctions (Bidding Agreements) Act of 1927. This states:

> If any dealer agrees to give, or offers any gift or consideration to any other persons as an inducement or reward for abstaining, or for having abstained, from bidding at a sale by auction either generally or for any particular lot, or if any person agrees to accept, or accepts, or attempts to obtain from any such dealer any such gift or consideration as aforesaid, he shall be guilty of an offence under this Act and shall be liable on summary conviction to a maximum penalty of six months' imprisonment and a fine of £100.

The operation of the ring is simple. One member of the ring who is established and financially important will be nominated chairman, and a local dealer will be appointed spokesman. The ring does not travel from auction to auction like a posse; it is formed spontaneously, most of the members know one another, and philosophically accept the fact that they are not the only ones there (one dealer and a flock of private punters is an unlikely Arcadia).

The spokesman has a catalogue with the lots to be 'ringed' marked. His aim is to acquire those lots at the lowest possible price, knowing that the big guns are not bidding against him. Or so he hopes. There may be a rogue dealer in the auction room who can outbid the ring.

After the sale, the members of the ring gather for the 'knock-out', in a pub or car-park, or anywhere where they can be assured of privacy. The goods obtained and paid for, are re-auctioned, with the chairman acting as auctioneer. Bidding starts at the price the lot fetched in the sale. Suppose this is £120, and the price reached in the knock-out is £300. The latest buyer pays out his £300, and the difference between the £120 and the £300 is divided equally among the non-buyers (making allowance for auctioneer's commission, of course—the spokesman has been repaid his full outlay). If several high-priced lots are bought by the ring, a member of a ring, even if he or she has bought nothing at the knock-out, can take away more than petrol money by simply being there.

Some dealers are more equal than others, and a few low-grade dealers and knockers join the ring simply to get a share of the take. If they are refused entry they can run the prices up and defeat the object of the ring. Not surprisingly, there is often a ring within a ring, from which knockers and the like are excluded. Bidding starts at the price obtained at the first knock-out, and the knock-out operation is repeated. Naturally this only works where there are high-quality antiques which warrant further exploitation.

The ring can come unstuck, often with amusing results. Through misunderstanding a ring can keep quiet while an outsider buys something at an auction for next to nothing, the corporate members of the ring being under the impression that the outsider is their spokesman. On one occasion at a London sale-room the ring tried to include two 'dealers' who turned out to be plain-clothes detectives.

Auctions themselves are 'clean'. Very few things are stolen on viewing day, and dealers almost never clear goods which they have not bought 'by accident'. With shoplifters so lively elsewhere, it seems surprising that auction rooms are relatively free from their expeditions. At country auctions security is very slack, with perhaps two or three elderly porters having the responsibility of watching over the goods.

There is nothing alarming about bidding at auction. One catches the auctioneer's eye with a raised catalogue or a hand, and once one is seen to be a buyer rather than a passer-by who has come in out of the rain there is no need to go into hysterics to attract attention. Auctioneers are seasoned professionals. They are not going to mark a lot down to you for blowing your nose. Their aim is to get through the sale at about ninety lots an hour with no interruptions.

For those with limited capital, it is important to remember how much one has spent. It is easy to overlook £10 here, £20 there, which can add up to a lot of money. And it is easy to overlook the actual mechanics of moving the goods one has bought. There is no point in expecting a massive Victorian wardrobe (bought because it was cheap) to go on top of a Mini with a roof-rack. Every dealer has done some impulse-buying at a sale room, despite innumerable resolutions to the contrary.

At an auction one has to make a spot decision on when to buy and for how much; everyone can have cold feet before the lot they are interested in comes up. Buying from other dealers is much more leisurely, and often reassuring. At an auction there is always the chance of being 'run up'. The running up can be done in various ways—by the vendor in the auction room pushing the price up by bidding himself, by an agent such as the porter, or by the auctioneer himself taking prices 'off the wall'—accepting non-existent bids in an effort to push the price up. Running up can also be done by a fellow dealer out of sheer bloody-mindedness, especially if one has acquired something which the other dealer was after.

When buying from another dealer, one knows what the price is and that it is often negotiable. Dealers expect another dealer to ask for the trade price. Sometimes the price accepted has no relevance at all to the price on the ticket. It all depends on the dealer, the price he has been paid for the article and what profit is reasonable; it may be 10 per cent less than the price tag, it may be 20 per cent less, it may be more. An average dealer often expects to 'double up' on small items under £4 or £5, and as an initial gambit might try for 300 per cent profit from a private 'punter'. Too strenuous haggling should be avoided. If the answer to 'Is that the best you can do?' is an uncompromising 'Yes' it is better to leave it at that, and buy or not buy at that price.

As with auctions, there is no substitute for a close examination of the item, using if necessary a watchmaker's glass (an invaluable accessory). With the advent of glass fibre, Barbola, and other do-it-yourself products, china repairing has become quite an industry. In figurines (the most vulnerable of all antiques) arms have been replaced, fingers repaired, and heads stuck back. In almost all cases, a repair can be discovered, but often only as a result of a close examination. Some dealers will volunteer the information that there has been a repair; but some will not, and some will simply not know.

Nothing should be taken on trust; first appearances can be deceptive. If a desirable oil painting is seen, make certain that it is not an oleograph (a print imitating an oil painting), if a water-colour is seen make certain that it is not a print, if a book is seen make certain that it is complete and, if it is illustrated, ensure that it has all its plates. Do not trust sight alone. It is easier to detect a flaw in china and glass by ringing it with the finger-nail or rubbing a finger-tip over the surfaces than by a visual examination.

Occasionally it is necessary to make a rapid assessment, for instance at street markets where hesitation may mean another buyer jumping in flourishing bank-notes. If one buys damaged goods, it is hard luck; a sale is a sale, whether it is from an auction, a dealer, or a private seller. Buying from private sellers offers the most chance of getting something really out of the ordinary. Items switching between dealers—dealers of the middle range, not the élite of Bond Street—tend to be antiques of the second order, simply because the cream has been sifted off by the top dealers and the rich. A private house can contain *anything.*

In dealing with private sellers one has to adopt a moral line, that may or may not be reciprocal. It is simply not done to 'stitch up' a private seller—i.e., to offer a trivial amount for something very desirable. This kind of sharp practice has given many antique dealers a bad name, and hardly a week goes by without a newspaper reference to some crafty dealer who has offered £20 for, say, a Georgian table worth several hundred pounds. On the other hand, a dealer who prices something at £10 that is worth £100 is a fool. A more perspicacious dealer deserves to take advantage of him. An antique dealer is not in the business for his health. He expects to make a fair profit on what he buys from a private source.

All this may seem to savour of hypocrisy. The private seller, it may be postulated, will ask what is thought to be a reasonable price for the items he is selling. But in nine cases out of ten a private seller will not specify a price, but will expect the dealer to make an offer. The dealer has to be both buyer and seller; this puts a heavy responsibility on him, for several reasons. The majority of private sellers are elderly, often need the money desperately, and have no conception of present-day prices. An old woman living on her pension or a fixed income from shares can consider £16 to be an enormous amount of money, even today when it is merely the price of a good meal out for two. The kind of elderly people selling their antiques are the middle and the old upper classes. They are the most bemused members of society. That they should be taken advantage of is not only grossly unfair, but rather unpleasant.

And taken advantage of they are. They should be given a fair deal and, to do them justice, most decent antique dealers do just that.

More often than not, the private sellers who have a price in their mind are those who have *Lyle's Price Guide* in their bookcase, have watched *Going for a Song* on television, and reckon that they know a thing or two. Often, their asking prices are inflated—'top whack' as it is called—higher than the dealer would go except at a top auction room. They have often shopped around, looking at the price tags on objects similar to their own in antique shops, and expect the same less a nominal 5 per cent or so. They become indignant when told that their asking price is out of the question. Buying from private sellers is not all sweetness and light.

Sometimes the private seller is more unscrupulous than the most grotty dealer. Goods claimed as perfect can be damaged, and they may belong to someone else (even a husband who happens to be out of the house). Always make a list of everything bought privately, and always obtain a receipt for the money paid, with the pieces itemized. Cash rather than cheques will be expected more often than not, and the acceptance of a cheque is refreshing evidence that one is trusted.

A private seller will either take goods to the dealer's shop, or telephone the dealer and arrange an appointment for him to view if furniture or large objects are involved, but all the private sellers who come into the shop may not be what they seem. They may be dealers pretending to be private sellers, or they may be thieves. It is difficult to spot a thief, and if there is the slightest doubt in the dealer's mind there should be absolutely no question of buying. Dishonestly handling stolen property is a crime. Receipts should be asked for, and a name and address. It is a good point if the seller accepts a cheque; a thief will not.

If the hopeful vendor is a thief, the goods offered for sale are most likely to be silver or jewellery. Good silver (worth more than £50) should not be bought in the shop unless its history and the circumstances surrounding it have been enquired into. Run-of-the-mill jewellery (up to £30) is easily stolen and equally easily disposed of.

If a thief is difficult to identify, so, often, is a dealer masquerading as a private seller. Some do this because they think they will get a better price, for dealers are inclined to overpay private sellers; the fact that the items are 'fresh' gives them an extra interest. Not that it matters much. A seller is a seller, under whatever colours he may be flying at the time.

Newcomers to the trade should not be too distressed by the fact that there are dishonest people and thieves about. The vast majority of buyers and sellers are honest, and it is a pity that they have to be regarded with suspicion because of the occasional bad hat.

Many dealers advertise for antiques in the local papers. The response varies, depending on the paper and the money laid out. The average seller will prefer to deal with someone with a big block advertisement than with someone who can only afford a two-liner. The reasoning is that a dealer who can afford £50 on advertising must be a successful person who knows the score and will give top prices.

Some dealers advertise that they do house clearances. Before offering to do this, a dealer should study the implications. A house clearance means that the dealer offers a lump sum for the entire contents of a house. A clearance comes up after a death. It is all very well if a dealer who does clearances can pick and choose, but a house clearance means just that. The rubbish, the soiled bed linen, the carpets, the kitchen debris, the battered wardrobes no one wants at any price, all must be taken away, if necessary to the municipal tip. It is hard work, and many dealers prefer not to know, though there are junk men who will agree to take the dross after the best of the contents have been creamed off.

There are complications about house clearances. Sometimes the person who receives the money turns out to have no right to sell the goods at all. The death of a relative often brings out the worst in people; they descend on the goods and chattels, and argue about what they want. It is not uncommon for a dealer to view the contents of a house, make an offer, which is accepted, pay out, and on returning to the house to clear it find that the better items have mysteriously disappeared, in the boot of someone's brother's car. It is wise when undertaking a clearance to meticulously make an inventory, and either pay when the goods are being collected or get hold of the keys.

Newcomers to the trade should be very chary about undertaking house clearances. It is easy to see a house crammed with goods and offer a high price, only to discover on closer examination that there is very little that is worth while. And, as with buying at auction, there are the sheer mechanics of carrying the job out—possibly the rental of a van and the hiring of a strong lad to do the humping. There is always the danger of over-estimating one's own physical capacity in one's eagerness to get the job done. This is one of the reasons why the antique dealer's ailment is often a slipped disc.

There are dealers with many years of experience who have never carried out a house clearance, and have never wanted to. There are some who never advertise at all. But advertising can pay, though one must not be surprised to find that the replies are not flowing in as plentifully as one expected. It is difficult to compete with the big advertisements put in by dealers who buy shipping goods, and it is, therefore, more profitable to concentrate on more out of the way items, or on just one object of a common type. One dealer advertised for chairs, and was inundated with replies from casual readers who never read the block advertisements of the shipping dealers but who happened to spot the request for chairs. Everyone has chairs. The dealer was not particularly enamoured of chairs, but sets of ordinary dining-room chairs fetch silly prices and there is always a chance of being offered something unusual.

There are various ploys for a dealer to use. Advertisements can be straight-forward, or they can be cunning. Some dealers unashamedly begin their advertisements 'Private collector requires . . .' believing, often correctly, that many members of the public would prefer to deal with a collector than with a dealer. Some newspapers have a 'trade' and a 'private' rate, and oblige the dealer to put name, address, and telephone number in the wording. However, this cannot prevent the dealer using his or her home address and posing as a private advertiser. Some dealers use artful or soothing patter, reckoning that this puts a prospective seller off-guard, though there is no way of knowing whether this approach works. A dealer who has found a formula will not disclose it.

It sometimes happens that a dealer pretending to be a private buyer receives a response from a dealer pretending to be a private seller. The spectacle of two dealers pretending to be clueless can be amusing.

The strengthening of the pound against the dollar has raised new possibilities. Many specialized British dealers are now buying in the United States, both from shops and at American auctions, which are a branch of show business. They can be puzzling to a dealer used to British auctions where decorum usually holds sway. The American auctioneer is an entertainer as well as a businessman, and he presents his goods as if they were cabaret acts. When there seems to be a lack of interest in certain lots he will switch his attention to others, often skipping a hundred lots, returning to the duller items when he has built up enthusiasm elsewhere.

In Britain an auctioneer is obliged to declare an interest in those goods put in by himself or by the auction room for which he works, but in parts of the United States this is not so, and where an auctioneer is pushing hard it may be for an entirely selfish reason. In the United States buyers at an auction are given a card with a number, with which they bid, and names are not used. A quaint feature of American auction room practice is that bids of over a certain amount (say $1000) are greeted with applause, a practice encouraged by the auctioneer, who will do almost anything to keep his audience involved. Invitations go out all over the country to interested parties and, for example, an auction room in Texas will be the centre of a city of caravans and mobile homes inhabited by people who have been persuaded that three days in a sale-room is a good way of passing their time. An experienced auctioneer will vary his performance by singing a song, or by impersonating a tobacco auctioneer.

As Britain appears destined to ape the United States in everything pertaining to entertainment, no doubt singing auctioneers will one day make their début at Sotheby's and Christie's.

Of course, there is no point in buying antiques at an American auction if the same kind of thing can be bought in Britain at a similar price. The articles dealers buy in America are American antiques that are seldom seen in Britain or on the Continent, and with the increasing importance of the Continental market an antique dealer from Britain may be acting merely as an agent, arranging for American goods to go to the Continent with their stay in Britain only a formality.

There would be more British dealers shopping in America but for the expense of transporting cargo. By air-freight the cost is 80 cents a pound, plus packing. Overland and by sea, the cost is a little less, but this method takes much longer and goods may be further delayed by strikes. Packing is very expensive, and for a large container the packing alone can cost a $1000. Small articles can be posted: the limit is 22lb. For jewellery and similar items this method is quick, convenient, and cheap.

The time will probably never come when 'ordinary' trade goods are bought in the United States by British dealers, and this is even truer of antiques bought on the Continent, though again specialist dealers can and do attend continental auction rooms and buy from continental antique shops. In most countries of the Common

Market there are few problems about buying and transporting the goods through customs. Between some countries there is often no need even to stop at borders. The only country which is more than perfunctory with regard to its own antiques is France. The French wish to keep their antiques in their country, an almost unique phenomenon. If this were the attitude in Britain the antique trade would be a shrunken thing indeed.

6 Presentation and selling

There are people who can sell and some who find it difficult, even embarrassing. It is much easier and less frustrating selling to a fellow dealer than to a private 'punter'. A dealer may be brusque, but is rarely rude. A private buyer can be rude about the goods offered for sale, about the shop, and about the price ('I bought one of these in Woolworth's ten years ago and it cost half a crown'). There are a range of about half a dozen stereotyped comments that can drive a sensitive dealer mad. Among them: 'My mom had one of those and she threw it away'; 'I wouldn't give it house room'; 'Some people might like these old-fashioned things, but I don't'. Many people, especially tourists, regard antique shops as mini-museums, somewhere to go to eat their ice-creams and get out of the rain. The dealers are curators who are expected to dispense information about every item that strikes the eye.

A dealer must be prepared for time-wasters and messers, and retain his good humour. A time-waster may surprise one, and buy something, or be a potential private seller. Appearances can mislead. A scruffy hippy one has marked down as a probable shoplifter can turn out, when he opens his mouth, to be a silver collector looking for saddle-back spoons. A little old lady with a string-bag full of dog food can have serious designs on a £300 grandfather clock. The prosperous-looking man with a Mercedes parked outside and with the apparent intention of bidding for the entire contents of the shop may be looking for a cheap enamel saucepan.

The dealer must also be prepared for the occasional oddity, even the occasional lunatic. Most of them are harmless, will say their piece, and go away. But it is worth bearing in mind that one day one may turn nasty, and to make contingency plans accordingly. It may be possible to make an arrangement with the owner of the neighbouring shop that a shrill whistle blast or a banging on the wall means trouble. Drunks can usually be humoured, by suggesting that there is more action up the road and that an antique shop is a pretty dreary place for someone bent on having a good time. Opening an antique shop in a fairly lonely area may have its attractions, but the dealer, especially if operating alone, must consider his safety.

Smart aleck dealers with big ideas can be very tiresome, as can runners. The latter are not averse to gently bullying, offering ridiculous prices, particularly if the dealer happens to be timid and a little on the aged side. If such behaviour becomes too aggressive, the man concerned should be told to get out of the shop and, if he refuses, the dealer should rush into the road and shout for help. There is nothing a runner wants less than a brush with the local law.

Foreign dealers are usually very easy to deal with. Although they often drive hard bargains, they are almost always courteous and if they intend to buy they do not mess about. Their dealings are usually in sterling. If they do not speak English very well they are often accompanied by a courier or 'jockey'. A jockey plans the day for the foreign dealer, he lines up an itinerary, and generally smoothes the dealer's way. Many of the jockeys are paid by the foreign dealer, while others are employed by shipping companies, which not only deal with carriage, packing, and the paper work, but pay the British dealer. At first glance, a jockey may be just another member of a group of visiting dealers, but if one person in a party does all the talking and translating, the odds are that this is the jockey. Sometimes they expect a rake-off, often a small antique such as a print or a modestly-priced piece of china; a commission of 5 per cent of the total sale is reasonable.

The dealers from abroad with whom the average dealer feels most affinity are Americans, mainly because they speak the same language. The bigger American dealers are a delight to do business with, but they are a tiny minority compared with the pseudo-dealers who have business cards printed and expect to cover their air fare by a bit of dealing. They often come on cheap package tours and expect a lot for $5.

Outside London, the foreign dealers most often met with are Dutch and Germans, with Belgians, French, and Italians as runners-up. The Japanese are big spenders in London, but do not appear to have extended their operations into the provinces.

The antique scene on the Continent is totally different from that in Britain. There are far fewer shops, and the trade does not depend on knockers and runners. Much of the dealing takes place at fairs, and nobody bothers much with junk and the lower echelons of the trade. A German antique dealer can make more money at the yearly Munich Fair than he makes during the rest of the year.

It is usual for foreign dealers to make regular trips to Britain, and it is worth while for a dealer to cultivate good buyers. If the price is right, foreign dealers are loyal.

For dealers and private customers, British and foreign punters, there is no ideal way to sell. Some dealers try to corner the customers and overwhelm them; others leave them to their own devices, letting them browse. There are three basic approaches that the customer may adopt: 'Have you any Goss china / double-headed pennies / Derby / medals / microscopes, etc.'; 'Do you mind if I look around?'; or complete and utter silence. Dealers favour the last approach, especially those annoying ones who enter a shop, scan the stock with glittering eyes, and depart. In general, the dealer should be unobtrusive and not appear over-anxious to sell; civil yet not over-familiar. A few words about the weather will establish a willingness to be sociable if the need arises. The goods in the shop should speak for themselves, and their price tags should voice their availability.

Some dealers prefer not to price their goods, but instead employ a code. It is a matter of opinion whether this is good or bad; it stops the shop being used as a three-dimensional price guide by browsers, but it can also deter people. Asking the price of something might seem to indicate an interest in buying, and many customers dislike the hard sell that might follow. More private people than one might imagine find it hard to say 'No, I don't want it'. They prefer to say, 'I'll think about it'.

There is also the implication in not pricing that the dealer is making a mental assessment of the customer. Will he or she put out £25? (The price of the same object to a dealer is £12.) Is he or she a soft touch? Many dealers refuse to go into shops where prices are not displayed.

Where price-tags are used, there will often be another figure—the trade price, often abbreviated to T1 or T2 (the stated price less £1 or £2) or −T1 or −T2, or even, in the corner, 1 or 2. There are shops where the owners proclaim, often in the form of a sign, that they do not give a trade price to anyone. In putting price tags on objects it is better to use tie-on labels than stick-on ones. Stick-on labels can fall off, or they can be switched. Certainly unscrupulous dealers have been known to go into shops and, while the owner's back is turned, they have switched labels. They are more inclined to do this when they know that the owner is out, at a sale or buying, and someone else is looking after the shop, someone who will not realize that a certain object is grotesquely under-priced when it is brought to be wrapped. Stick-on labels can also damage the object to which they are stuck, leather and silk are especially vulnerable to such damage; when they are removed the labels often pick up the surface of the material.

Presentation can be important, though older dealers often have a 'reverse sell' technique which involves piling their goods around and on top of each other, a procedure in which dust and grime play their parts. Sometimes, however, a merry jumble merely means that the dealer no longer has the strength or the inclination to display his wares. This approach is seen at its zenith in old-established second-hand bookshops where the effort to collate and shelve the books is too much for the owner.

Silver and silver-plate, old copper and brass can be transformed if they are cleaned. Small silver articles can be cleaned in a few seconds by being immersed in 'silver dip'. Furniture should be clean, but be selective about strenuous polishing. China and glass collect dust; not only are they more aesthetically pleasing when clean, but a layer of dust indicates that they have been in the shop some time, and no one likes to buy an object that has been passed over by many other customers.

There are certain parts of the shop that, without apparent rhyme or reason, are selling places. It is a good idea to swap goods which seem to stick around, to see if a fresh location will help them on their way. The window is, of course, important, particularly in attracting the attention of private buyers. It should remain lit at night. Not only because light deters burglars, but also because it often happens that a passer-by sees something in the window after shop hours that he or she will return to buy the following day. The window should be tiered, using shelving or graduated blocks of wood so that the goods on display are on different levels. What-nots and display stands are very useful, either in the window or near it. An easel is an excellent way of drawing attention to a particular picture. There should be a variety of objects in the window, including unusual eye-catchers, and it is always advisable to have a notice stating that the owner wishes to buy antiques, listing some of the kinds of things wanted. The notice should be clear and competently done, and should preferably be set in an attractive picture-frame.

Some dealers prefer to place a small selection of their better stock in the window, but this can deter the less affluent who may feel that if this is the class of dealer there is no point in going into the shop. All depends on where the shop is; in a select prestigious area, a display of high-priced antiques may reap a reward from those who only visit *la crème de la crème.*

As far as display inside the shop is concerned, there are many options. However, there should be no obstacles: the dealer should be able to see all parts of his shop at a glance. Objects should be placed so that they are not likely to be knocked over by the clumsy customer; small expensive items should be kept in locked cabinets or cases, which are opened on request; furniture should not jut out, tripping customers or banging their elbows; if pictures are shown, they should not be hung too high on the walls, as this prevents easy examination. If books and postcards are on sale, they should be positioned so that browsers do not block the shop.

Grouping or mixing the stock is a matter of personal choice. A colourful mixed display can prove more interesting than a group of items of one sort bunched together. Much depends on the space available, and on the amount of stock.

Some dealers display a sign stating that all breakages must be paid for. This may or may not act as a deterrent, but has no force in law. Breakages do not *have* to be paid for, and if some accident does occur this fact should be borne in mind. The general public is divided into two groups: those who are very embarrassed by the damage they have caused and will pay, and those who will simply disappear into the street.

Opening and closing times, stated perhaps on a notice on the door, should be adhered to, though dealers are notorious for opening and closing their shops as and when they feel like it. Many dealers close on Monday, feeling that this is traditionally a slack day, but it is advisable to stay open on Mondays for the dealers who take this day off use the time to go out buying! It is expedient to go along with the half-day closing of other shopkeepers in the town. A passing dealer, realizing that this is the half-day closing, will not bother to find out if the odd antique shop remains open.

A corner of the shop should be retained as office space, housing a desk, reference books, takings book, and labels. Wrapping paper should be kept near at hand, as should cardboard boxes in which bulky or fragile items can be packed.

There is no set profit margin for antiques. In selling to dealers it must be remembered that they have to resell at a profit, and so anticipate them making at least 20 per cent. Trade discount when selling is usually a minimum of 10 per cent, but this is negotiable, as in buying.

There are fewer considerations in selling from a stall at a fair or market, but items should still be displayed in an attractive manner, using shelving and wood blocks to provide several different levels. A general rule is to place larger items at the back of the stall and smaller ones at the front, with jewellery or silver being kept under constant supervision. Articles of jewellery should be pinned to a mount covered with velvet or some similar material, though junk jewellery up to £3 in value can be placed in a large bowl for customers to browse through. Fragile and vulnerable articles should not be placed too near the edge of the stall.

A refreshing feature of markets and fairs is that there is almost always a much larger volume of passing trade than one gets in a shop, though the percentage of buyers may be less. Sales can follow in a fast and furious manner, especially when the market opens and the dealers are waiting to buy. It is wise to have a piece of card handy to jot down the sales as they occur. When no one adheres to opening hours, the dealers will be crowding around as the stall-holders unpack. The main thing is not to get flustered; if there is something they want they will not mind waiting a couple of minutes. At fairs and markets most of the transactions will be in cash, and the stall-holder should have plenty of change.

Dealers buying at fairs and markets expect prices to be flexible, and stall-holders feel less obliged to price their goods, leaving it to the whim of the moment. Experienced stall-holders know what they have paid for everything on their stalls, and expect to make less profit on individual items than shopkeepers do, making up the money by the greater volume of sales.

It is sometimes advantageous to have relatively few items on the stall, so that the buyers' senses are not surfeited. It is often amazing how a stall-holder with a dozen items can clear half of them in a matter of minutes, while much the same objects on another stall in the same market remain unseen and unbought, overwhelmed by sheer numbers. Of course, the dealer who uses this gambit must have other stock in a box beneath the stall in order to replace the goods sold.

A stall-holder should use the space available to the best advantage, and it is advisable to take a small tip-up table or two to fill in any gaps between your stall and the next one. Larger objects can be displayed in front of the stall.

As markets are a free peep-show there are more potential customers at them than at fairs, where there is usually a small admission charge. The majority of the visitors, however, have no intention of buying anything that costs more than 50p, and it is all a mystery to them. People interested in antiques and anything old have little conception of the blandness of taste of most of the population. This is a fairly recent phenomenon dating from the 1950s, when prosperity began to afflict—and the word is deliberately chosen—the working population. Before then, people lived with old things out of necessity—their parents' furniture, hand-me-downs of all kinds. The coming of the supermarket brought plastics and so-called contemporary furniture and furnishings into their lives. It is therefore understandable that this generation—and the one that has succeeded it—might be looking at the artefacts of Ur for all the sense antiques and bric-à-brac make to them.

This is sad, but the fact remains that selling old things to these people is like selling ice to Eskimos and their lack of interest in the items on the stalls does not reflect on the intrinsic value of the articles. They are the non-speaking extras in the antique game. It *can* be depressing if dozens of people pass by without a glance, but it is inevitable. At least visitors to antiques fairs are interested enough to pay their 20p admission fee.

With outlets such as fairs, markets, and shops, why do dealers sell through the auction room? Most of them do at some time or other, and a high proportion of the goods in an auction will have been put in by the 'trade'. The most obvious items put in are those that are sticking, but there are certain pieces which do better at auction than in a shop, especially specialized antiques which appeal to a minority—the more obscure scientific instruments such as inclinometers, art pottery by obscure but collected makers, and ethnographica which to the casual passer-by looks nothing.

Then there are those antiques that the dealer is frankly at a loss with. They *may* be worth a considerable amount of money, but they are out of his field and he has no idea what price to put on them. Such articles will find their true level in the sale-room. The auctioneer's advice can be very helpful in these cases; he not only has a wide knowledge of antiques in general, but also has a fair idea of the prices the most diverse objects will fetch. He will also be able to suggest a realistic reserve price. This is important, for if the reserve is set too low and there are no knowledgeable private buyers or out-of-town dealers present at the auction the dealers' ring may be able to snap the item up cheaply.

Another advantage of selling at auction is that in times of financial stress one can put a large number of items in and recoup one's outlay within a few weeks. Large provincial auction rooms hold fortnightly, monthly or bi-monthly sales. Specialist items put into a London auction room may have to wait longer, until a suitable specialist sale comes up. A disadvantage of selling at auction is that the hoped-for profit is cut into by the auctioneer's commission, which usually varies from 10 to 15 per cent. If an item does not reach its reserve, most auctioneers make no charge, but when selling at auction rooms with which one is unfamiliar it is advisable to check this when entering goods.

It is sensible to put reserves on all the items put into an auction, even goods the dealer hopes to see the back of. Lots without reserves are sometimes grouped together and sold as one lot, and this can—though not necessarily—result in a lower price being obtained than if the goods were lotted separately.

As with buying at auction, it is a good idea to scout around before putting goods into a particular auction room. The vast majority of auctioneers are above reproach, but one does not want to see one's goods given away. One can do that oneself.

The auctioneer usually provides a printed form for the vendor to fill in. The vendor writes down the items he or she intends to put in, with a reserve; the vendor also states his VAT number, if he is registered for VAT. The auctioneer does not give the vendor a copy of this form, so it is advisable to make one out oneself. Even experienced dealers often find it difficult to remember what exactly they have entered in a sale. Prior to the sale, the auctioneer sends the vendor a copy of the catalogue, in which his lots are specified.

It is a matter of temperament as to whether or not the dealer should turn up at the sale and try and boost the items put in. This is all right up to the reserve figure, but unless one is experienced it is possible to buy in one's own goods inadvertently, and there is something very depressing in being saddled with something one had intended to get rid of.

7 The scope of the trade

It is no good buying something that no one wants. It is a general rule, however, that an object of quality will always sell. But what is quality? Is there inherent quality in one material, and an absence of it in others, such as plastic, or does quality reside in the appearance of the object or in the workmanship involved in making it? It is worth thinking about this, though the considerations will not be consciously taken into account. Plastic, for example, was skilfully used in the 1930s in Art Deco jewellery, often in combination with exotic stones and metals. The appearance of an object can be in flat contradiction of the workmanship. Whatever one might think of the tasteless, tortuous designs of Indian screens and tables, there can be no question of the quality of the workmanship.

And what is workmanship? Among the most saleable of antiques is late Victorian oak furniture (known as 'pussy oak' because of the delight of the designers in incorporating lions' faces in the furniture). Much of this furniture was mass-produced and machine-made. There was no delight in craftsmanship as the worker used his mechanical saw. Yet there can be no question that much of this late Victorian oak is quality furniture.

The result of the antique explosion that began in the mid-1960s is that certain categories of antiques have priced themselves out of the reach of the average dealer. Consequently attention has become focused on hitherto neglected items. This is especially true of furniture. After World War II there was a run on Regency furniture, and in more recent years Victorian furniture has had what many feel to be more than its fair share of attention. As the popularity of Victorian furniture zoomed—far more than Regency furniture did in the late 1940s and early 1950s—so attention shifted to Edwardian furniture. The most recent development has been the evaluation of good furniture of the 1920s and 1930s, where there is still great scope for an unprejudiced dealer. Georgian and pre-eighteenth-century furniture has always been in fashion, and always will be.

Some antiques have become over-expensive, but it is a fallacy that good furniture is not available to the average dealer, considering the circumstances. During the boom in Victoriana, certain kinds of furniture were neglected. As the Davenport and the chaise longue doubled and quadrupled in price, so ebonised furniture, arts and crafts furniture, and bamboo furniture languished. They still have to reach their logical places in the pecking order. More incredible still, while the trade was going mad over Victoriana the superb quality of Edwardian reproduction furniture was overlooked. When, after a long pause, this furniture was belatedly taken up, *art nouveau*-influenced furniture remained in the doldrums (as the more homely examples still do).

Booms and fashions are not logical, but the trade responds to what is trendy and acceptable, whether it is gracious living (Georgian and Regency) or phoney simplicity (stripped pine, brass, and copper). It is up to the individual dealer to take advantage of inconsequential changes in taste. In the past, furniture that has come into fashion and then gone out of it has gone on the rounds again. The Victorians demoted Georgian furniture to their servants' bedrooms, the Edwardians threw out their Victoriana, and in the 1920s and 1930s contemporary furniture came in. G-plan seemed to its owners to render everything else old-fashioned and passé.

When the enormous export business in antique furniture is taken into account it is not surprising that large quantities of furniture are lost for ever. It is difficult to estimate how many antiques have gone abroad; there are no figures available, nor are there ever likely to be. The furniture has been sealed into its containers by the exporters, the contents unknown to all except the vendor, the consignee, and the innumerable officials who stamp little bits of paper. To some members of the trade, it seems as if everything has gone. But the number of antiques in private hands in Britain is still immense, and notwithstanding the prophets of doom, never-ending.

During the late seventies the antique exporters suffered a number of setbacks, and there is good reason to believe that a strong pound has stemmed the flow. Nations, other than the British, have run into economic difficulties. Doubtless there will always be ups and downs, but some antiques are actually being brought back into Britain. Certainly the shippers (the antique exporters) are more cautious in their buying after the halcyon days when anything with a couple of knobs on was worth three times its London price in Sydney, Amsterdam, or Hamburg.

This is not of purely historical interest. The shippers no longer rule the roost in the auction room, and 'shipping gear' or 'crud', the wash-stands, hall-stands, chests of drawers, and drop-leaf tables of mediocre quality are beginning to find their own level as utilitarian objects of no great appeal. Anyone can buy them, if one wants them. The caution now shown by shippers has hurt the 'runners', who bought for them exclusively; it has also hurt some dealers, who built up a collection of shipping gear for the shippers and runners to pick up.

Many of the irrational spurts in prices that have occurred have been due to sudden demands by the shippers, and as their requirements work their way through the trade a good deal of mental adjustment takes place. With the shippers now being more fussy, it can be unwise to buy goods with them solely in mind.

Although furniture is the staple commodity in the antique business, there are many dealers who never touch it, particularly the specialists and those who have no shop outlet. The importance of furniture is a phenomenon dating back no more than sixty years; prior to that, paintings were far more important.

Profit margins on paintings can be immense, far greater than on furniture where the higher the quality and price, the lower the percentage (it is not out of the way for a shipper to buy a piece of furniture at £600 and sell it for £625). Fairy stories connected with pictures abound: in 1977 a picture bought for £38 at auction was resold the week after for £3000. In the same year, a print bought at an open market for 50p proved to be a Goya worth several hundreds. Picture dealing can be a continuous adventure story.

With so much money at stake, it is not surprising that forgeries and fakes abound, and the signature, which should be the least important element of a picture, is regarded with awe even by experienced dealers who should know better. In the nineteenth century, when painting was a leisure activity favoured by young gentlemen and ladies alike, the standard of competence among amateurs was very high. All art was representational, and the amateurs took as their models the current masters, especially of landscape. In the fullness of time these amiable creations have acquired the signatures of sought-after artists. An innocent copy or pastiche has become a not so innocent fake.

It is easier to obtain knowledge about pictures than about any other category of antique. The standards of reproduction in art books are very high indeed, and it is much easier to minutely examine paintings at art galleries than it is to examine porcelain or furniture in museums, for it is essential to handle the latter objects to get the feel of them.

Honest-to-goodness pictures are very reasonably priced, particularly water-colours. There is assumed to be something high class about oil paintings, and a hopeless daub can command more than a good quality water-colour. The price is often subject to the content of the picture, not to the way it is painted. Sea pictures are always good sellers, and so are aircraft, trains, and cars, where accurate representation is more important than age. Landscapes in which not very much is happening can stick, even when well painted and 'like'. City and town scenes are always preferable to rural landscapes. Oil portraits and 'full lengths' are very saleable; pretty women and handsome men are preferred (a uniform is a decided plus). The trade cannot get enough sporting paintings to satisfy the demand, and sporting prints are healthy, though many fine eighteenth- and nineteenth-century prints were reproduced early in this century and it is sometimes difficult to pick these out. Interiors, even when splendidly done, can be hard to sell; church interiors, of which there are very many, are the worst of all. Genre scenes are perhaps the best of all, whether they are of farmyards, streets or people carrying on their business.

Landscapes are always more saleable if they contain water, even a modest duck-pond, and tranquil scenes are more acceptable than stormy ones. This applies to sea pictures as well. Flower paintings, surprisingly, do not sell at all well, yet this is a sphere in which the amateur excels (but for every good flower painting there are a dozen shockers influenced by van Gogh's 'Sunflowers').

Except for those depicting sporting subjects, and naval and military actions, prints remain under-valued. Even on a pound to pound basis, coloured prints after Reynolds and others are less expensive now than they were during the heyday of the print seventy years ago. Even good-quality eighteenth-century sepia prints can be picked up for a few pounds (and framed, at that). Modern reproductions have induced a state of uncertainty among buyers. Hand-coloured fashion plates are perennial sellers.

Modern art, except perhaps in London, is out. The only kind that sells at all is traditional representational art, preferably painted in minute detail. Animal paintings are always in demand, but buyers expect absolute realism, especially in horse pictures, and the amateur who can get away with landscapes and architecture often stumbles when it comes to putting life into a puppy's eyes.

Old animal pictures, however, can be almost comically inept and still sell.

A dealer who has recently opened a shop will inevitably be approached by a local artist asking if he or she can display a picture in the shop to be sold on commission. It can be a delicate situation, because the picture is more likely to be bad than good (a good artist has probably found outlets already). It can be tactfully pointed out that the shop is for antiques only, and that modern paintings do not fit in. If the painting is good, there can be no objection. The usual rate of commission charged is between 10 and 20 per cent. This applies as well to general antiques put in on a sale or return basis.

If the antique shop is in a beauty spot or a tourist centre there will certainly be a market among the visitors for local prints. These may be old black-and-white prints hand-tinted, or modern reproductions, and so far as the average tourist goes they are all one. It is up to the individual to decide whether he wishes to deal in commercially-produced prints.

One of the better places to buy paintings with a view to reselling is the medium-range antique shop. General dealers prefer to turn their stock of pictures over fairly quickly for the simple reason that pictures take up valuable wall space and only a limited number can be displayed at any one time. Dealers who have no shop and rely on fairs can arrange to have their stalls backing on to an inner wall rather than in the centre of the room, so that they can arrange to bring peg-board with them. This is ideal for displaying pictures. Dealers who attend open air markets should be very chary of pictures; a sudden downpour can ruin their stock in a matter of minutes. Rain penetrates the backs of framed watercolours in a manner not far short of magical (oil paintings are less vulnerable, and can be wiped dry without ill effect).

At some stage or other, the dealer will have to face the fact that inadvertently he has bought something that is a reproduction, whether it is a modern engraving or reproduction copper and brass. At one time, reproduction copper and brass was wafer-thin, shiny, and thoroughly nasty, but now more thoughtful makers are turning out brass and copper complete with the signs of wear and having the weight of the old articles. Moulded brass no longer has the tell-tale coarse finishing that we see in cheap horse-brasses. Favourite brass items are 'Victorian' door-knockers and letter-boxes, and 'old' car-horns. The presence of great blobs of solder on copper and brass does not necessarily indicate age. Of course, there is no reason why a dealer should not deal in honest reproduction brass and copper—the 'mark up' is high—but the presence of reproductions in a shop can have two effects. Firstly, it may indicate to a buyer that the the dealer has bought the reproduction objects believing them to be old; secondly, if the copper and brass are reproduction, other things may be too. For example, there is a flourishing industry in 'old' wine-glasses (pontil marks and all), and it often needs an expert to differentiate between excellent modern Chinese porcelain and the old.

The newcomer to antiques can, if he or she allows it, be in deep water over porcelain and pottery. There is so much to know, and if a dealer can differentiate between the products of three periods (pre-Victorian, Victorian, and twentieth century) that in itself is a good start. The first rule of the thumb is that anything marked 'Made in England' is twentieth century.

There are three basic books a novice dealer should have: *Lyle's Price Guide*, a handbook of silver marks, and a good handbook of pottery and porcelain marks, such as that by Geoffrey Godden. The only snag is that not all pottery and porcelain is marked, and some of the most desirable and expensive pieces have no marks at all, while run-of-the-mill stuff is often crawling with them, from makers' full names and addresses to pattern numbers. In the ordinary way of business, a general dealer will be confronted by hundreds of different pieces and will gradually learn from experience what sells and what does not. Even reliable firms such as Royal Doulton and Worcester produce ware that simply does not sell, but gathers dust on the shelf.

Because there is so much pottery and porcelain about, newcomers to the trade tend to get lumbered with it, and stall-holders can find, to their dismay that it forms up to 90 per cent of their stock. There they are, the uninteresting shaving-mugs, the tureens, the jam-pots, the biscuit barrels, and the pairs of vases. In the course of time, they acquire chips, which renders them even less interesting.

The lesson is: do not buy pottery and porcelain because it is cheap. It is cheap because it is plentiful. Do not buy incomplete tea-sets, do not buy large plates and dishes (unless they are blue-and-white and have a recess), do not buy anything chipped or cracked unless it is earlier than about 1850 or very pretty, and do not pay more than £2 or £3 for pieces marked 'Made in Czechoslovakia' or 'Made in Japan'. 'Made in Germany' is all right; the Germans did a lot of quite intricate commemorative and seaside stuff, known in the trade as kitsch, which is quite saleable. You can buy ugly things if they come from an art pottery; art potteries had a God-given right to produce ugly things.

All this would, no doubt, seem impertinent to a dealer in fine porcelain, but there is no question that to the average dealer the high prices obtained for certain pieces of porcelain is incomprehensible. A plain white Chinese pot valued at several thousand pounds creates the same kind of confusion as the fact that modern paintings, which take less than half an hour to complete, are worth similar sums of money; there seems to be no correlation between the object and the monetary value put on it—unlike furniture and period paintings.

In one sense, fine porcelain is the ultimate antique. It is functionally useless and expensive because it is rare. It may be beautiful, but not necessarily so.

One of the hardest tasks facing a newcomer to the trade is to decide whether porcelain and pottery figures and figurines are old or new. A glance in the window of a good quality gift shop will show that modern firms are producing splendid porcelain figures at much less than £10 each. There is nothing shoddy about them, and the only objection to them is that there are tens of thousands of them about. In pottery, there are Toby jugs, pairs of crock dogs, and Staffordshire figures and groups (known as flatbacks—the backs are plain and undecorated). It is often difficult to differentiate between those made a hundred years ago, those made forty or fifty years ago, and those made yesterday. It is certain that anything which becomes trendy will be reproduced by manufacturers who will use the same techniques and materials as their predecessors. The more recent examples of this are pot-lids and Victorian fairings. As soon as a piece of antique pottery tops £100, whether it was given away or sold for a few coppers when it was first made, the reproductions begin to appear. This happened in the 1960s with porcelain thimbles, which went round the trade at between £10 and £15; there was suddenly a glut of them, modern replicas retailing at less than £5.

Of course there is a world of difference between manufacturers jumping on the band-waggon and honestly selling 'antique' pot-lids and fairings, and forgers aiming to pass off their products as the genuine article, sometimes even acquiring the original moulds.

The best advice to dealers offered what at first appear to be valuable pieces at a knock-down price is beware. In other categories, one can weigh up the chances of something being reproduced in common-sense terms. No one in their right minds would reproduce a Victorian walnut what-not or rosewood table; even at £200 or £300 the cost of reproduction would be prohibitive. No one would reproduce an Edwardian Chippendale-style cabinet. But intricate porcelain is not much more difficult for a skilled firm to make than ordinary cups and saucers. Workmanship as a criterion for determining what is genuine and what is reproduction does not work.

Furniture, paintings, porcelain and pottery are the staple commodities in antiques, but in all kinds of antiques it is worth asking oneself: is it genuine? is it worth reproducing? is there an easy way to tell? has there been some recent fashion to focus attention on something hitherto neglected?

There are thoroughly safe categories. Paintings, whatever signatures they bear, are one-offs and need skill to do them. So are sculptures. There must be a question-mark against bronzes, as they are moulded, and there can either be original moulds at large, or moulds can be made from old fashionable bronzes (such as Degas dancers or the animal bronzes that have become so popular recently). The advent of cold-cast bronze adds to the uncertainty (compressed bronze powder is used). *Art nouveau* graphics, especially posters, must be very suspect. However, scientific instruments of the eighteenth and nineteenth centuries would be too expensive to reproduce, as would period clocks and watches.

Every newcomer to the trade buys clocks, as they seem astoundingly cheap. And some are, but unfortunately they are the ones no one is terribly keen to buy. The most prolifically spawned clock is the Victorian mantel clock, which usually appears in marble, slate, or simulated marble. Some of them are quite impressive, but even so they do not command much money. Their price to shippers is no more than £15 apiece. Westminster chimes clocks dating from the 1930s are also about in large numbers; their going rate is no more than £8 or £10–less than their cost when new. On the other hand, Victorian hanging clocks and grandfather clocks–properly called long-case clocks–are always in demand. Early clocks are very much the specialist dealer's preserve.

It is very easy to date clocks; they look their period. There is one exception—the carriage clock. The modern carriage clock is almost identical to its predecessor of more than a hundred years ago, and if it is tucked away in a corner and has acquired a layer of dust it can easily arouse false hopes.

Watches are always saleable—at a price. With the virtual extinction of the pawnbroking profession, watches are constantly being taken to antique shops to raise pin-money, and a dealer has to make a rapid off-the-cuff assessment. Wrist-watches are relatively modern, and are resold for use rather than as antiques. It is advisable to keep an eye on jewellers' windows to keep in touch with modern prices, and the offer made should be dependent on the maker's name —Omega, Timex, or whatever. It is easy to overpay on watches brought into the shop, and even a good quality second-hand watch will rarely be worth more than a quarter of the jeweller's shop-price. If a private seller is asked if the watch is in going order, the answer will usually be yes, irrespective of whether this is true or not. Long-standing faults cannot easily be detected by a non-expert, but if the watch keeps good time for five minutes—down to a second—there is usually nothing much wrong. It is advisable to keep an accurate watch in the shop as a time-keeper.

Wrist-watches that do not go, or that lack a winder (the usual fault), must be valued on their scrap value if silver or gold. The scrap value of silver is negligible.

Pocket watches are a different proposition. The basic types most often met with are gold and silver Hunters and half-Hunters, and modern pocket watches of the Ingersoll kind. Hunters have a silver casing at the front and the back, half-Hunters have a casing at the back only. Older watches are much more interesting. Fusée-drive watches have a tiny chain wrapped round a core instead of the conventional mainspring. Makers' names and intricately engraved watch-plates inside are a decided plus; there may even be watch-papers tucked inside the back; these are themselves collectable. However, really valuable watches are rarely toted round to antique shops by the kind of people who own really valuable watches.

The most frequent items brought for sale to a dealer are not watches, but jewellery of one kind or another. An antique shop is probably not the best place to take jewellery, but somewhat surprisingly the average dealer will give more than a jeweller, even when the jeweller charges a high price when reselling. For jewellery in an antique shop is cheap, often ridiculously so. Often this is because the dealer is not quite certain of his ground, and does not know whether he has or has not got jewellery of any value at all. It is easy enough to find out about gold and silver by simply reading off the marks, far less easy to differentiate between diamonds, imitation diamonds (paste), and diamond-like substances such as spinels, not to mention the multitude of precious and semi-precious stones. In buying jewellery, there is also the problem of differentiating bone from ivory (the only sure way is to set fire to it—ivory does not burn), or amber from plastic or jet from black glass (jet is lighter in weight).

Many dealers would rather steer clear of jewellery, but if someone comes into one's shop with *anything* the inclination is to buy it rather than turn it down. As with almost every other antique item, the seller rarely asks for a price, but more often than in any other category jewellery has been valued, and an expected price is often this valuation. Hardly anyone brings in a written valuation or is certain of the identity of the valuer, and it hardly needs to be said that a valuation for insurance purposes has no relevance to the market value of the jewellery under appraisal.

The purchase in the shop of jewellery brought in by a stranger is fraught with problems, the main one being the possibility of it having been stolen. Most middle-range jewellery is anonymous; on the police lists one reads 'gold ring with diamond'. It may state the carat, but with the best will in the world the police can hardly be more precise. A diamond ring, or even a diamond cluster ring, is difficult to describe in more than half a dozen words.

Learning about jewellery is not only helpful in business, but is some insurance against buying valuable jewellery for a nominal sum. A jewellery thief does not necessarily know the value of the jewellery he or she has stolen. A dealer who has paid £20 for a box of what he thought was costume jewellery but which proved to be worth more than a thousand pounds will, unless he looks an absolute moron, have some awkward questions to answer if the police interview him.

Male thieves often send their women accomplices into antique shops to sell their ill-gotten gains, as they know that a woman selling jewellery is more convincing. It is a favourite way for hard-up women to get pin-money, and even poor-looking women do have good jewellery.

There is no guaranteed way to tell a wrong 'un. Appearances are deceptive. Everybody who comes into the shop with jewellery to sell must be treated with a certain amount of suspicion, unless they are local and known to the dealer. If in doubt, if there is something that strikes a wrong chord, do not buy.

The odds are that thieves trying to sell their stolen goods to an antique shop are small-time or amateurs. The professionals have their regular outlets, 'bent' dealers and fences. Silver is an especial target of thieves, particularly burglars, but it is only rarely that an ordinary dealer is approached with valuable stolen silver.

Silver-buying is not such an uncertain business as being obliged to make spot decisions about jewellery. The prices of silver are fairly well established, and the price guides perform a useful office. A book of silver marks is very desirable, though if the dealer is caught without one it is comforting to know that a man's head amongst the silver marks indicates that it is Georgian (a useful pointer to novice collectors who may not have run across much silver).

As with jewellery, the most unlikely people can own silver. A silver tea-pot can be handed down as a sort of tribal memento in families where furniture is sold and anything else antique is dismissed as old-fashioned. The item most often brought into a shop for sale is cutlery, and it is important to remember that, for example, Victorian tea-spoons are common. It is easier to over-pay for silver than for any other kind of antique.

Experienced dealers are never confused by silver-plate, but some good quality silver-plate is adorned with very impressive marks, and even the E PNS can be served up in fancy script. Silver-plate has a modest role in the antique hierarchy, and the salvers and trays are only interesting if they are heavy and have some feel of quality about them. Many private sellers honestly believe that E PNS (electro-plated nickel silver) *is* silver; it is not. There is no silver in it at all. There is one category of collectable plate, known as old Sheffield plate; this is silver on copper, applied mechanically and not chemically (as more modern silver-plate is). Old Sheffield plate ages picturesquely, with the copper showing through.

Plated Britannia metal is very common and not much sought after. Britannia metal has a fair age to it; it is a poor man's pewter, but when the plate is wearing it can look very nasty. Pewter itself is an entirely different matter. Old pewter has a sturdy look about it, and it has 'touch-marks' to show its provenance. Books about silver marks usually have a section on pewter marks; to most general dealers, pewter is an unfamiliar area, and it is worth while getting to know a little more about it as it is still under-rated, except for the really old chargers (large pewter plates). There is an immense amount of pewter about dating from the turn of the century; some of it is rather dull, but this period has come into its own, and anything 'characteristic' is most collectable.

Wooden objects are known as treen, a rather silly word derived from the word 'tree' and defined as 'small articles of wood, especially eating and drinking vessels of past times'. There are ardent collectors of treen, and any dealer who wishes to know more should go and see the Pinto Collection in Birmingham Museum. There is a surprising variety of objects in this field. Many of them are quite plain, but this does not detract from their desirability. Modern wood wears just as equably as old wood, and kitchenware of the 1930s might well pass as treen. It is not a category known to the general public, and there is little likelihood of treen being brought into a shop. It is a fairly old collecting category, but there is plenty of room for new dealers to specialize in it. It is a 'safe' subject, as it has never been too trendy and prices have not become ridiculous. Overseas buyers have not shown much interest in it.

There are types of antiques that have become so over-exposed that to all intents and purposes they have disappeared from the general scene. One of these is old dolls. There was always a limited supply of good quality dolls, but they have received so much coverage that they have become rare objects, only within the province of museums and very rich collectors. This has happened before. In the early years of this century there was a sudden flare-up of interest in leather bottles and drinking vessels that drove them off the market into private collections and museums. Now, a general antique dealer can go through life without ever coming across leather bottles and drinking vessels.

There are also types of antiques where collecting fever is rampant. A good bookshop will indicate these areas (a real collector will always buy books on his or her subject). They include militaria, postcards, postage stamps, miniatures of all kinds including model cars and dolls' house furniture, anything nautical, scientific instruments, coins, needlework objects, and anything to do with cricket and the more esoteric sports (a handkerchief commemorating W. G. Grace sold in September 1978 for several hundred pounds). Such a list can be almost endless. A point to remember is that a keen collector with hours to spend on a subject will know more than the normally well-informed dealer. When a collector enters an antique shop he or she hopes to find an ignoramus; collectors can be as sharp as the most knowledgeable dealer.

Collectors will often leave their cards, and may tell the dealer that they will buy anything in their field. As in other cases, it is never wise to buy especially for one person, whether it be a shipper or a collector, as there is a chance of disappointment. What may be unusual and exciting to a dealer can be commonplace to a collector. A stamp collection full of exotic varieties, for instance, may be turned down with a sneer by a philatelist. If one is dabbling in coins or stamps, a current catalogue is essential. On the face of it, an American silver dollar looks as though it is worth money (considerably more than a dollar), but they are very common and do not command more than £3 or £4 each. And spectacular coins are worthless if they are defaced or have been soldered to something to make a brooch or an ornament. Contrary to popular belief there is no real money in Victorian pennies, farthings, or threepenny bits, except for odd ones of a particular year (which are correspondingly rare and have a habit of not turning up in job lots of coins).

Medals is another field where caution is advised. Literally millions of medals were issued during World War II; millions more were issued in World War I. Their rarity value is usually nil. Common-sense will always help in case of doubt. A minor Victorian war means fewer medals issued, and the subsequent guarantee of them being relatively rare. A working knowledge of nineteenth-century history often helps a dealer in more ways than one.

Every dealer, experienced or novice, will have a rush of blood sometime, and be taken in by some glittering bit of nonsense. It is part of the fun and the uncertainty. The main thing is to be able to afford an excursion into the unknown, and to shrug it all off if it goes wrong.

8 Transport and packing

Buying and selling keeps the antique merry-go-round turning, but apart from dealing a person in antiques has to think of all the ancilliary activities. Some of them are mundane, but they can be important, and failure to take note of them can result in irritation and may be expensive.

First of all, there is the question of transport, and an antique dealer without a car is working at a disadvantage. If the dealer buys anything big there will be the cost of delivery. A private customer can sometimes be accommodated; if the profit has been sufficient, a dealer will trundle the goods up to the purchaser's house. But a dealer is expected to do his or her own fetching and carrying. A dealer in small items such as jewellery is not so inconvenienced by not having his own transport; a small hold-all can contain all his purchases, and most of his stock. There are some jewellery and silver dealers who travel around on motor-cycles.

Many people going into antiques in middle life, perhaps with a redundancy payment or a golden handshake, or with savings accumulated over the years, will already have a car. Is it the right kind of car? A Rover may be all very well for an executive, a sports car may be ideal as a week-end runabout, but are they functional? Most cars are. The average dealer will be handling items that fit perfectly well into the boot of a car or on the back seat, and furniture will pose the only problem. The answer is simple: a roof-rack.

The best kind of roof-rack for a dealer is one that covers most of the top of the car. Most cars except soft-tops and sports cars can take a roof-rack. It is easy to put on, and equally easy to take off. The only disadvantage of a roof-rack is that one cannot use a car-wash machine at a garage. It is also inclined to whistle at high speeds, and shudder slightly, but its value can hardly be over-estimated.

It is much less irritating to put a piece of furniture on a roof-rack than to attempt to manoeuvre it into a car, even if it fits. A roof-rack is at a convenient height, and there is less chance of cricking one's back or slipping a disc hoisting a heavy object on to a roof-rack than with struggling with it into a car. It is easy to over-estimate one's strength when handling furniture. What seems reasonably light at first can, after a minute or two, become unbearably heavy. To lighten the load, drawers should be removed from chests-of-drawers and other furniture. When the piece of furniture is to be put on a roof-rack, all bits and pieces such as ornamental knobs should be removed.

The climate plays a big part in the antique dealer's life. The sun can send people into a shop or market, and so can the rain. When arranging to move furniture on a roof-rack a weather eye on the sky can save a lot of aggravation. Solid furniture such as oak will come to little harm, but quality mahogany or anything which is veneered can suffer terribly in a downpour. Large sheets of heavy-duty polythene should be carried in the car.

The furniture should be securely tied on. Some dealers use elasticated ties with metal hooks at the end, but these tend to become stretched after wear. Strong rope is useful, but where it meets the furniture it should be padded with rags or pads of news-paper. Better than elasticated cable and rope are the canvas ties that are used by furniture removers. These can be drawn taut across the furniture without damage.

Obviously most movement of the furniture in transit is back-wards and forwards, but the most dangerous is the sideways move-ment caused by strong winds, and it is important to take this into account not only when tieing it on but also when arranging the furniture. There is no one way to arrange the ties, but slack should be taken up by feeding in extra ropes or ties; it is better to be laborious than casual. The ties should not be fixed to the roof-rack so that they slide along the bars—the most useful part of the roof-rack is the unit fixing it to the rims on the roof of the car.

The furniture itself should be utilized when tieing up. Chests-of-drawers can be held rigid by tieing around bun feet, chairs can be slotted into each other, and an upturned table can provide a stable platform for smaller pieces of furniture. It is important to see that there is no rope hanging free, and the furniture should not protrude excessively at the front or back as the police take a dim view of this.

Better than a car with a roof-rack is a van; second-hand vans are usually a lot cheaper than second-hand cars, and if the dealer is thinking of a trade-in on another vehicle, a van should be considered.

Pottery and bric-à-brac in general, are known in the trade as 'smalls'. They are best carried in cardboard boxes (easily obtainable at the nearest supermarket) and the secret of safe transit is to pack tight. Even the most fragile pieces of glass will travel well if wrapped in newspaper and packed tight. Unless they are exceptionally fine pieces, brass and wooden items need not be individually wrapped, but more attention should be paid to copper and especially pewter, which is a very soft metal. Tiny items should be placed in a small box or other receptacle, as when unwrapping it is easy to overlook very small packages.

Packing and unpacking is one of the chores associated with fairs and markets, but it is amazing how quickly it can be done with practice. It is advisable when packing to have plenty of old newspapers available, so that one is not forced to economize. Tissue paper, bought in commercial quantities not sheet by sheet, is also extremely useful, not only for packing but for wrapping up goods for a customer. It is also handy to have polythene carrier bags. A buying dealer, loaded up with purchases, is apt to look kindly on a seller who provides a carrier bag and is likely to come back again.

When purchasing really large pieces of furniture ('lumps') the cost of transport should be taken into account when working out a reselling price. There are always one-man firms with a van or lorry looking for work, but for some items a specialist has to be brought in. Large mirrors should not be left to the amateur, nor should pianos. Moving pianos can be expensive, and it is simply not worth while looking at ordinary cottage uprights with a view to making a profit on them. It is not surprising that very large pieces of furniture without anything much to commend them except their size are inclined to stick.

Car expenses, and especially the cost of petrol, are almost certain to be the largest item for a dealer to budget for. A stall at a one-day fair a hundred miles away may seem cheap at £15; but petrol to and fro could cost another £12 or so. It is easy to overlook these hidden expenses when pricing one's goods.

9 Cleaning and simple restoration

An antique of almost any kind looks better for being clean, and it is important to know what cleanser to use. In general, proprietary cleaners do their job very well—Goddard's Silver Dip for silver, Brasso for brass, and the various types of Duraglit have much to recommend them. Soap and water can never be improved upon for certain tasks. Soap and water clean amber, horn, and tortoiseshell. Ivory should be sponged with water, but never soaked. Gold can be cleaned with soap and water, and finished off with jewellers' rouge, a polishing powder of hydrated ferric oxide and a useful all-round agent. White marble can also be cleaned with soap and water, but care should be taken with coloured marble. Petrol may be used for coloured marble, and also for alabaster, which is often confused by the tyro with marble, which is much harder.

Ammonia is a reliable stand-by. It helps to remove the tarnish on silver (but not on bronze), and when added to warm water is ideal for cleaning porcelain and glass. Strong ammonia is a good varnish-stripper, rather less brutal than some of the proprietary brands. Brass can also be cleaned by using a solution of ammonia, followed by a vinegar and salt mix. Bronze should be treated with some caution; after a time it acquires a patina that adds to its attraction. This patina is the result of corrosion, and in early bronzes it is much prized. Sometimes a patina is so desirable that it is faked, by making a solution of copper nitrate and salt, applying it, and following up this treatment by applying another solution made up of 100 parts of weak vinegar, 5 parts of ammonium chloride, and 1 part of oxalic acid, which is repeated when the bronze is dry. After about a week the effect of this treatment will be apparent. Unfortunately for fakers, this kind of deliberate patination is easily detected as it is spread too evenly over the surface of the object. True patination is erratic.

Pewter can be polished with whiting or silver sand, but being a very soft metal nothing too drastic should be attempted, especially if it is old pewter as the 'touches' or makers' marks may be damaged. Iron should also be treated with caution, using fine wire-wool and oil. Cast-iron seems to be more vulnerable to rust than wrought-iron, and a nice piece of old cast-iron can be reduced to a pile of bits by cavalier handling. Until recently, articles of iron have been the poor relations in the area of metal antiques, but now they are beginning to make a showing.

Objects which have been buried for a long time often acquire a limestone accretion that does not seem to yield to ordinary cleansers. Ancient coins are typical of this kind of category, but other small items can also benefit from the following treatment. The visible surfaces are coated with paraffin wax, and the object is then dipped into concentrated nitric acid, which will attack the limestone deposit but against which the wax protects the good surface. Immersion time depends on how the acid is working. When all the limestone has been taken off, the wax is removed and the object is washed in running water.

The severity of treatment depends on the value of the antique being treated, and it is a good idea to practice on something that is worthless, though metal objects can usually take a good deal of rough treatment. Metal is sometimes varnished, even polyurethaned, and it is always advisable to get rid of this varnish as it invariably detracts from the character of the metal. It is a matter of opinion whether the lacquer applied to brass when microscopes and other instruments were made should be removed. There are many proprietary varnish-removers, but acetone is as good as anything. If, during the course of the operation, one changes one's mind it is useful to remember that kerosene (paraffin oil) will stop the action of the acetone.

Circumspection is necessary when dealing with more fragile materials, such as porcelain, pottery, and glass. Common-sense tells us that soap, or liquid detergent, and water are ideal cleansers for pottery and porcelain, always provided that the objects are glazed. Plaster of Paris should never be touched with water, nor should gesso, which is the substance found on ornate picture-frames. Surface scratches on glass can be removed by using a chamois leather impregnated with jewellers' rouge, and cloudy glass can be cleaned by being immersed in distilled water to which 5 per cent sodium hydroxide has been added.

A problem often met with is a cloudy deposit inside a decanter, which is impossible to reach even with the cleverest bottle-brush. Decanters belong to a class of antique bought for use rather than decoration, and a dirty looking interior puts buyers off, especially private buyers. There are two methods that work. One involves swilling coarse sand around, and the other involves using lead shot, of the kind used by anglers.

Cracks in porcelain and pottery have always been something of a problem. One authority advises rubbing the cracks with cotton-wool dipped in bleach (it is the dirt in the crack which shows, not the crack itself). Professional china restorers find it easier to cope with chips than with a crack. A more drastic remedy is to immerse the cracked object in household bleach (such as Domestos) for a week or so, but pieces of value should not be submitted to this treatment as the bleach seems to have a habit of biting into pottery and expanding the cracks into something like ravines. Once a piece of china or pottery has a crack one must accept it. And that applies to glass as well. It is worth noting that there is a dealers' trick to 'cure' a crack in glass. Placing a glass under running water causes the crack to disappear as if by magic—until the water in the crack dries. So if a dealer says: 'Oh, yes, I have an old drinking glass in the back that might interest you . . . I'll just go and fetch it . . .' the would-be buyer's response must be one of caution.

An over-enthusiastic approach to the cleaning of silks, fabrics, canvas, paper, parchment, or leather is not to be recommended. The cleaning of pictures is an art in itself, not to be treated lightly, and a picture of real value should have expert assessment. An oil painting can have its varnish removed with no great alarums and excursions; artists' colourmen such as Winsor and Newton market an excellent picture cleaning fluid. The main thing is to stop when the cotton wool suffused with the cleanser begins to show signs of paint.

Newcomers to art restoration will be surprised by the amount of varnish there is to remove. Stripping varnish off a picture can be a messy and lengthy business, and a speculative buy at a pound can turn out to be an evening's hard work. There is a happy side to speculative buys, however; picture canvas is so expensive today that an artist or art student will invariably give a dealer a profit on an oil painting bought on spec for a pound or two.

Oil paintings always deteriorate. The canvas, the paint, and the varnish are all subject to the ravages of time. The most that can be done is to stem the deterioration for a time. Surprisingly, most oil paintings are fairly resilient, and can stand a good deal of trial and error meddling, and an oil painting with a value of less than £30 can be worth restoring by the average dealer with an hour or two to spend.

Crackle is not so detrimental as one may fear, and even has a prestigious French title, *craquelure.* It seems to give an indication of age, so much so that modern forgers spend a good deal of time putting crackle in, either by rolling a canvas or using an 'ageing varnish' which conveniently breaks into a network of small lines. Crackle can also be painted on, using a very fine hair-brush.

Crackle only becomes sinister when it develops into cracks and fissures, which in turn lead to flaking.

As with cracks in china, it is not the crack itself that is ugly but the dirt accumulated in it, and cleaning may very well take some of the grime away. For pictures with cracks in which flaking is ready to occur, a clear varnish in an aerosol spray may well settle the surface, but for pictures in which flaking has started it is vital to get the bits stuck on firmly as soon as possible, and a little work at this stage is preferable to repainting a section that has fallen off. An oil painting, of course, is not protected by glass, and a chip of surface paint is lost when it has become detached from the rest of the picture.

Where flaking is ready to occur, it may be advisable to delay cleaning off grime and dirty varnish until the surface has been stabilized. This is done by making a mixture of 75 per cent beeswax and 25 per cent resin, and dripping it on to the flaking area. Over this is placed a layer of heat-resistant silicone paper. The mixture will quickly set, and it is gently melted while the flaking surface is stroked flat with a palette knife. A thermostatically-controlled spatula is available to professional restorers, but an ordinary hair-dryer makes a good substitute. After this flattening operation, the silicone paper and any residual wax is removed with the aid of white spirit. The beeswax and resin mixture acts as an adhesive and as a binder. It is possible to use more modern methods, but the use of instant adhesives will make it difficult for any future restorer.

Blistering can be tackled in a similar way, by injecting the mixture into the blister with a hypodermic syringe and pressing down the surface with a palette knife under heat. Wrinkling, where the surface has taken on the appearance of tiny wavelets, is more of a problem. Usually this happens because overpainting has been done before the underpainting is dry, or because varnishing has been carried out too quickly (at least six months should elapse before a painting is varnished), or, most probably, because the varnish has been applied too thickly. The best solution is to take the varnish off, and see if that eliminates the wrinking. In any event, if it is the paint surface on which the wrinking occurs, a fresh varnishing will make it less evident, and may hide it completely. Good quality paintings are rarely subject to wrinkling; if the cause is the paint surface, it shows haste and indifference on the part of the artist, who deserves all he or she gets in the way of obloquy.

Bulging and sagging are not so serious, unless their effects are evident in flaking. The sagging may be the result of wedges coming adrift from the stretcher on which the canvas is nailed (wedges are always provided on good quality stretched canvas to keep the surface taut). The answer is to provide new wedges, cut from a bit of firewood. If the old wedges have become slack and are not performing their duties, they can be replaced or supplemented with mini-wedges. If the sagging is not caused by wedge-trouble, and the stretcher seems to be unwarped and symmetrical there is one way to set about curing it, though it is cavalier and should only be practised on a picture of modest value. The painting should be removed from its stretcher and placed face-downwards on a blanket with an intervening layer of waxed paper. Hardboard is then cut to the picture size and laid on the back of the canvas. Weight is applied to the back of the canvas (one restorer uses three layers of concrete blocks). The same result can be obtained with less hard work by the use of strategically-positioned clamps.

All this may seem to demand an extravagant amount of time and effort, but unlike many antique restorations and renovations, picture restoring can be fun, and at every stage one can see the progress being made. In few other spheres can one make something of nothing. A barely decipherable canvas picked up from a pile of rubbish pictures may turn out to be something worthwhile.

The job that sounds the most daunting of all in art restoration is lining, but like most things the process is less formidable if one finds out what exactly art restorers mean when they speak of this with awe as the ultimate. Lining is simply dealing with a canvas which is in a bad way. There are two types of lining. The easiest form involves attaching a fresh canvas to the back of the old one. The painting is taken off its stretcher and examined carefully. If a painting needs lining the odds are that the edges have frayed and decayed, and the lining canvas should be cut a little larger so that the rotten borders of the existing canvas can be trimmed. The painting is placed face downwards on a flat surface covered with a blanket, and the canvas is sandpapered to provide a biting surface.

The lining canvas (bought in rolls from an art-shop) is stuck to the old canvas with an old-fashioned adhesive brewed up in a double glue-pot and made up of:

16oz (454g) beeswax
12oz (336g) resin
4oz (112g) paraffin
3oz (84g) turpentine

This makes a sticky, pungent but malleable substance akin to thin treacle, and it is painted on the back of the original canvas and the toothed side of the relining canvas. The two canvases are pressed together, with the aid of an electric iron set at warm. The mixture may press through damaged canvas, but this does not matter; it can be removed at leisure with a warm blade of a knife. If the existing stretcher is all right, or can be renovated, the double canvas can be tacked back. This form of lining is uncomplicated and not difficult to do.

The other form of lining is far more drastic, and demands a certain commitment and confidence. It is only practised when the canvas is virtually falling apart, and the aim is to replace the original canvas with a new one, leaving the painting intact. This might seem a contradiction, as it is obvious that the painting is done on the canvas. But an oil painting consists of at least two layers, and often three or four, particularly when the painting is old and painted in the traditional way.

The first thing to do is to fix the painting surface. This is done by pasting on alternate layers of cotton sheeting and newspaper or paper towels, using a simple flour-and-water paste. One begins with a layer of cotton, and several hours should elapse between the application of each cotton and newsprint layer, so that each is absolutely dry. When a quarter of an inch (60mm) of sandwich is built up, the canvas is scraped using a sharp-bladed knife or a fine wire-brush. Odd bits of canvas that have become imbedded in the paint can be left. A canvas in decent condition would take many hours to strip off, but as this kind of lining is only attempted where the canvas is in a bad way it will not prove too arduous.

When most of the old canvas has been removed, the painting itself is bonded to the new canvas using the beeswax and resin mixture described above. All that remains is to remove the layers of canvas and newsprint, and this is done by using a wet sponge and taking off each layer separately.

When lining has not been carried out but there is a hole or two to repair, this can be done by glueing patches to the back of the canvas and repainting. The best medium to use when repainting is attempted is one which is rather sticky and thick, such as copal medium. This will bind better with the existing surface than a more transparent lighter medium. Attempts at cleverness should be avoided; the aim is to make what was a hole less conspicuous. A fresh coat of varnish will complete the operation. Some professional restorers go overboard on varnishing, and put on as many as six coats. On olde-worlde paintings, perhaps painted only a few years ago with intent to confuse, there is sometimes an intervening coat of coloured or stained varnish (and sometimes a coating of size to further deter curious restorers).

Water-colours are rarely varnished, and if they are their value drops dramatically. Damp is their enemy. Damp damage most often occurs in the areas bordering on the frame, and as most water-colours are mounted before they are framed there is always a good chance that the damp will stop before the water-colour is reached. The damp mark on a water-colour might seem easy to take out by simply taking a camel-hair brush loaded with water and going over the edge of the stain, hoping to match the two areas of colour. All too often, this will create a new stain. Painting over and applying a fresh wash, slightly darker than the original, may be tried. But a good painting is good because the artist was an expert, and amateurs' well-meant restorations are glaringly apparent.

Much depends on where the damp stain is. If it is in an unimportant area of sky or a part of the picture where nothing much is happening the picture can be 'cropped'. That is, the water-colour can be made smaller by increasing the size of the mount (always remembering not to crop the signature, a talisman even for those who should know better).

Annoying as damp stains are, foxing is even more irritating. 'Foxing' refers to the brownish spots to be seen on prints, drawings, water-colours, and old paper in general. As the colour in most prints is fixed, the entire print can be immersed in a solution of moderately strong sodium chlorate, then washed in water, but obviously water-colours need more careful treatment. Every art restorer has a recipe, but a solution of hydrogen peroxide and alcohol applied with a camel-hair brush on the foxing is as efficient as any other method.

As most general antique dealers are middle-men for pictures, it may be advisable to relinquish all thoughts of restoration and sell oils and water-colours as they are, faults and all, and leave the work to someone further on in the chain, contenting oneself with wiping the dust and dirt off the frame and cleaning the glass. Where there is no running water available—e.g. in a lock-up shop —Windolene in aerosol form is admirable for cleaning off grime.

Whether the dealer does much to furniture is again his choice. Certainly it is important to freshen up a piece of furniture, not difficult with the wealth of excellent polishes and waxes available today. The standard polishing wax is Antiquax but many dealers prefer to prepare their own, with beeswax as the basic ingredient (three parts of beeswax to eight parts of spirits of turpentine). Sometimes it may be necessary to remove old French polish. A varnish-remover will do this, as will liquid ammonia with acetone (nail polish remover). Of course, this provides more work, though at one time there was a fashion for French polishing anything that stood still, even the most inappropriate objects.

A shining piece of furniture frequently sells to a private customer who simply would not notice it in a dirty state, but grubbiness does not put off a private buyer as much as woodworm, and woodworm holes should be dealt with as soon as possible. In old furniture the woodworm is usually dead, and then it is only a cosmetic operation. To make certain that one is not dealing with live woodworm, the furniture should be tapped gently; if a fine sawdust trickles out of the hole, the woodworm is alive and well and living in the furniture. The edges of the holes are also sharper and cleaner when live woodworm are present.

Live woodworm is not a major disaster, but it has to be treated instantly, not only on account of the furniture in which it is found but because there is a chance of it spreading to other furniture. Woodworm prefers softer woods, and mahogany is rarely attacked. Oak is also resistant, though this does not stop unscrupulous dealers from putting woodworm holes in 'old' oak—the faked ageing process carried to its limit. The holes of live woodworm should be treated with Rentokil. All holes should be filled, a favourite preparation being beeswax and turpentine, though a quick method involves the use of shoe polish (shoe polish is an ideal colouring agent for fillers of all kinds).

Whatever their do-it-yourself capabilities, most dealers will at some time or another try their hands at simple repairs—putting back a chair leg, replacing a broken chair stretcher, sticking down veneer which has lifted, or replacing a castor. The more enthusiastic and ambitious unglue old codged-up repairs in the belief that they can do better. Often they fail, and whereas an old repair is acceptable and can even—in the case of old oak or walnut—enhance the charm of a piece of furniture, a modern repair often kills a sale, just as surely as glistening modern French varnishing does.

If repairs are undertaken, it is important to use the right kind of wood, and preferably old wood, perhaps taken from a broken piece of furniture. Repairs and renovations to elegant furniture are usually outside the range of the average dealer, and there are certain woods that are almost unobtainable today (tulip-wood, zebra-wood, and even that most common Victorian wood, rosewood). Amateur woodwork is seen at its most inelegant in pine. Pine is a wood where delicacy of execution is neither expected nor possible, and a certain crudity is acceptable. Pine dressers can be fixed up with bits of wooden boxes (with the original wording stencilled on) and this does not seem to detract from them. The stripping of pine has become a major industry, catering for a trendy demand. The stripping process, carried out in a tank of caustic soda or by the use of paint remover, takes away the signs of age, and 'country pine' can be a hundred years old or made yesterday with few to argue about it.

Repairs that are in character can be spoiled by the use of modern nails and screws. Hand-made nails were being produced well into the nineteenth century, and every demolition yard has large numbers of them (though a demolition man will ponder on the sanity of dealers scrabbling through old wood looking for hand-made nails). Screws have altered far more; pointed screws did not come into use until 1851. Modern counter-sunk or round-headed screws can look ridiculous on an old piece of furniture. No restorer worth his salt will use screws on pre-Victorian furniture (screws were used extensively on Victorian furniture especially on household furniture such as wash-stands and sideboards), except where they are in character (as in tilt-top tables).

Screws and nails can easily be taken out, and the holes filled with plastic wood. Shaky legs should be glued, preferably with 'Scotch' glue, which is bought in cakes and broken into pieces. A proper glue-pot is essential for its use. This is a double pot, the inner section containing the glue, the outer the water. The glue is covered with water, and water is poured into the outer section until it is half-full. The pot should be heated on a slow heat, and when the glue has melted it should be applied thinly. Clamps or a vice should be used while the glue sets. The white woodworking glue marketed under various brand names is a tolerable substitute, particularly for smaller articles. An important feature of Scotch glue is that if the restoration goes wrong there is plenty of time to remedy it, and even when it has hardened the glue can be softened under heat. Araldite or other instant adhesives should be avoided; the dealer who does use them will receive no thanks when further repairs become necessary in the future.

A good deal of substantial furniture is pegged. No one expects the average dealer to do pegging or fancy dovetailing or mortice-and-tenon work, but the appearance of pegging if not the reality can be accomplished by sinking suitable discs of the appropriate wood into the surface.

There is no question that of all antiques, damage to furniture is the most easily rectified, and with this in mind it is well worth looking more closely at furniture that at first glance appears hopeless. A battered carcase can be turned into something nice. A decent enough table from which the veneer has all but peeled completely may be a worthwhile proposition; the veneer can be stripped off, and the solid wood beneath polished and made into an acceptable surface. Veneer which has 'bubbled' may look ugly, but it is easily remedied. One way is to cut the bubble lengthways and across with a razor blade or a scalpel, insert glue, and press the pieces back; another is to inject glue under the bubble with a hypodermic syringe, and then apply pressure (the glue residue will seep back through the hole).

A task which every amateur restorer faces at some time or other is the replacement of missing castors, and one is well advised to build up a collection of various types of castor from rejected or junk furniture. The most desirable castors from the restoration point of view are those made of porcelain or brass, though the composition castors used in the nineteenth century are also of use. Castors have a high casualty rate, and frequently break off at the disc which is screwed on to the end of the furniture leg. With the constant weight of wear, the screws have usually bitten deeply into the wood and are difficult to move.

The temptation is to keep on trying, until the screwdriver damages the slot, but before this stage is reached the screwdriver should be struck on the handle with a mallet. This often loosens the screw. A hot iron applied to the screw will make the screw expand; when it cools, it contracts, making removal simpler. Penetrating oil, such as Three-in-One, can also do the trick. No matter how much of a nuisance the screws are, one should never have recourse to brute force; if the disc is levered out there is a better than even chance of damaging the leg, as often a castor disc has a metal shaft in the middle which fits inside the leg.

So many private buyers these days try their hand at upholstery that chairs and settees with sagging springs, lumpy stuffing, and torn fabric often sell as well in their rough condition as they do re-upholstered. The spiral spring was an early-Victorian invention, and upholstery in pre-Victorian furniture is concerned with coverings and padding. The earlier the furniture the sparser the covering.

There is more stuffing than one might imagine in Victorian furniture, whether it is horse-hair, flock, or other kinds of padding.

Often it is filthy, though the full horror lies in the easy chairs of the 1920s and 1930s where everything is padded and which are better left alone. All furniture containing spiral springs is upholstered in the same way. Jute webbing is tacked criss-cross to a frame on the underside of the chair or settee. These carry the springs, which are tied to the webbing. Above the springs is the padding, usually inside a cushion, held in position by a covering of canvas or a similar material, and the chintz or velvet or Bri-nylon goes on top of that. The webbing is covered with a fabric to prevent dust getting in, a task it signally fails to perform.

Often a sagging chair merely means that the webbing has frayed or broken, and that the springs are poking through against the fabric covering. It is a simple handyman's job to tack on fresh webbing and re-tie the springs to it, remembering to keep the webbing taut throughout the operation. Old padding, especially horse-hair which has nothing to recommend it, should be thrown away; there are plenty of good modern materials, whether it be flock (made from refuse wool), kapok (a material substance from an eastern tree), or foam rubber.

Covering a chair can present rather more problems, one of which is that the colour the upholsterer choses will not be one that a potential buyer wants. A neutral green or a rust colour are middle-of-the-road choices that may satisfy, but the tastes of private buyers can be bizarre in the extreme.

Chairs and sofas in a reasonable condition otherwise can look grubby if they are grease stained. The Victorians invented the antimacassar, a cloth to protect chair backs from the macassar oil used by gentlemen as a hair-dressing. Unfortunately the antimacassar died out. Grease can, however, be removed by using petrol, alcohol, ammonia, or soap and water, depending on what sort of grease it is. Dry cleaning fluid (carbon tetrachloride) can also be used. Much depends on the material, and cleansing should be carried out with care. Petrol should never be used on silk. When dealing with grubby fabrics it is often better to have a clean sweep, and renew them rather than try to revive them.

If the dealer is doing anything with furniture there is room for error; wood is a stout material that can take clumsy treatment. Not so porcelain and pottery. Repair and renovation is tricky, and even those jobs that seem most simple may turn out to be time-consuming operations. The easiest job an amateur can do is to stick pieces of broken china together, or re-stick with instant adhesives those repair jobs that have been carried out using old-fashioned brown glue. One is sometimes tempted to remove rivets—the old way of repairing china when adequate adhesives were not obtainable—and make good using modern methods, but this can be fiddly. It is better to realize that with a rare old piece of china a rivet is acceptable, and make allowances for the repair when buying and selling.

With the range of fillers and clay substitutes available today there is nothing to stop a keen dealer from trying to make something of nothing, but it is not just a question of supplying an arm for a figurine, replacing a slice of plate, or fitting a spout on a teapot, for there is the colouring, and in particular the difficulty of matching up whites. The white from a tube is rarely the exact white needed, and a good deal of trial and error is necessary. The best kind of paint to use is acrylic, which is quick drying and can be used with both water and acrylic medium (which gives the paint more body). Glazes can be counterfeited by the use of clear varnish.

As a hobby china restoring has a lot going for it, but a dealer in serious business must wonder if the time expended is worth while. Often the answer must be no. One cannot stress too much that a repair is a repair, and a good repair will only deceive some of the people some of the time. It can be rash to send a well-repaired piece on its journey, for somewhere along the line some dealer will certify it perfect with ultimate dissatisfaction all round.

However, for dealers prepared to try their hand there are certainly more materials available for china restoring than was once the case. Perhaps the most versatile is Araldite, the makers of which have put on the market a range of products with porcelain and pottery restoration in mind.

In many cases the article which the dealer wishes to repair will be one which has already been repaired—badly. The first job is to undo the previous work by dissolving the adhesive, which is most likely to be an animal product. A hot compress applied to both sides of the join will usually do the trick. It is better to loosen one piece at a time, so that the process is controlled. A little detergent added to the hot water will help. If shellac was used as the adhesive, it can be softened by methylated spirits, again in compress form.

All traces of the old glue should be removed, and when this is done the pieces (and the body of the article) should be washed. The edges of the pieces should not be touched by the hand. The pieces and the article are then warmed; this guarantees that all moisture is removed, and causes the fixative to thin slightly, making an easier join. Araldite is then mixed according to the instructions on the packet. It is wise to think a little ahead. A simple break is no problem, but where an object is fragmented the individual pieces should be laid out on a soft cloth so that reassembly can be done more easily. If one knows where pieces are to go without fussing around, a few valuable minutes may be gained and one's patience may be less tried. Araldite takes some time to bond (even the quick Araldite), and while this is happening pieces can become relaxed and even drop off, so strips of sticky paper—½in (1.2cm) brown strip is the best—should be kept ready, together with a dish of water to wet them with.

If there are more than three or four pieces it is better to stick them separately, first of all choosing two pairs of adjacent pieces with long common edges. Join the pairs together to make two larger pieces (where there were once four). It is then necessary to wait (usually twelve hours) until the adhesive has bonded (or, more correctly, 'cured'). The process is then repeated until just two large pieces remain to be joined to complete the article. At every stage, excess adhesive should be wiped off, and the sticky paper carefully applied. When the object is complete, immersion in warm water will cause the sticky paper to float off. The use of paper strip serves two purposes; it keeps the pieces together until the adhesive hardens and also pulls the pieces tightly together as the water dries out.

Cracks can be dealt with by squeezing Araldite—thinned by warming—into the fissures, after the cracks have been cleaned. It is often advisable to make the cracks wider, so that cleaning becomes easier. The Araldite not only guarantees that the crack will not develop into a break, but provides a surface suitable for painting on.

Missing pieces call for more ingenuity, but a surprisingly good substitute for porcelain is a mixture of Araldite and titanium dioxide. It is rarely worth while making up a piece to fit into a missing plate or dish. Figures and decorations such as flowers, leaves, and tree branches are far more suitable. There are two ways of replacing missing pieces; one depends on the artistic skill of the restorer, the other on patience and perseverance.

The first method, in which one can see results as they happen, involves drilling the object and inserting a brass dowel of appropriate length, set in with Araldite. Then make a stiff mixture of Araldite and titanium dioxide (marketed by Parvane Ltd), and build up the missing piece in several applications, allowing each to set before going further. When an approximation of the missing piece has been achieved, final detail is applied by the use of files and abrasives.

The second method involves making moulds. This is most successful where there is something perfect to model from, such as a group with a pair of identical cupids one of which has lost a head, or a pair of figurines, one with an arm missing. It is not difficult to make a two-part mould using plaster of Paris. When the mould is hard, the interior should be coated with a wax. The Araldite and titanium dioxide mixture is then pressed into the two-part mould, and removed when hard, a task made easier by the wax coating. The casting will not be perfect, and will have to be smoothed with file, glasspaper, or abrasive stone. It will then be stuck on to the object, using the same mixture to hide the join.

For objects where there is no perfect match to provide an instant mould, the missing part can be modelled in wax. The only advantage this method has over the first, where the new feature is sculpted as it were on site, is that the wax piece can be altered and messed about with until it seems satisfactory. When the part has been modelled in wax, it provides the mould in plaster of Paris as before.

At this stage, the restoration will not look particularly impressive, even if the modelling has turned out well. The glazing provides the essential finishing touch. The recommended glaze to go with Araldite-based repairs is Chintex, which can be coloured with oil paint to the required hue, and is applied to the figure or article that has been restored and is then baked in an oven at 120°C for one hour. Above this temperature there is risk of discoloration. If in doubt about the effectiveness of an oven thermostat or if one suffers from nervousness a cold glaze can be used.

The fact that porcelain is glazed is something that deters amateur restorers. Unglazed earthenware presents fewer problems, in that missing parts can be restored using a mixture of powdered earthenware of a similar colour to the original and Araldite. If the appropriately-coloured earthenware pieces are not available, powder colour as used by young children at school can be blended into the mix. Earthenware itself is the cheapest of all commodities, and a chain-store will have an endless variety of mundane kitchen objects at a very reasonable cost that will provide a basic stock.

The glaze can be applied using a soft brush or by using an air brush, as used by commercial artists. An air brush is not cheap, however, and only fairly large scale operations warrant its use. Sometimes, depending on the object being restored, several glazes will need to be applied, coloured and uncoloured. After each application, the object should be baked in the oven.

Whether it is financially worthwhile for a dealer in serious business to go to the lengths of restoring china is a moot point. It depends largely on how one feels about china, whether restoring damaged pieces is a labour of love or whether china is just one more category of antique needing to be 'turned over'. But whatever one feels, a damaged piece is a damaged piece no matter how many man or woman-hours have been spent in trying to disguise the fact.

10 Account keeping

There is nothing complicated about keeping the accounts of an antique business, and provided that one jots down immediately all one's buys and sales one cannot go far wrong. With the best will in the world it is all but impossible for a dealer to keep business cash and private cash separate in pocket, or wallet, and so notes of purchases and sales need to be accurate even when, as at markets or fairs, buying and selling may be carried out at high speed. Small notebooks, preferably hard-covered so that they do not disintegrate, are ideal for on-the-spot transactions.

The basic books for an antique dealer are as follows:

Purchases Book in which to record date, seller's name, item, and price paid
Takings Book in which to record date, item, and price obtained
Cash Book which should be double-columned
Diary
Invoice Book essential if dealer is registered for VAT
Ledger optional
Petty Cash Book
Expenses Book

So far as keeping track of the progress of the business, the cash book is the most important account book. One's purchases are entered, with the date and seller's name, in the first column. When the items are sold, the price obtained is set in the second column.

A three column cash-book can be used if required, with the profit set out in the third column. This multi-purpose cash book also serves as a stock book, with the items unsold being abstracted, as well as a handy reference book. If the items are described in detail, the buying and selling prices will provide valuable information at some time in the future.

Even when it is tiresome, small items such as pieces of cheap jewellery in the £1–£2 range should be set down separately. It is very difficult to describe jewellery succinctly, and it helps if each new piece of stock is given a number, this number appearing in the cash book alongside the item and on the price tag. The removal of the price tag when the article is sold also serves as a check.

Many dealers keep a diary in which everything is put down—sales, purchases, expenses, and also the names and addresses of people with whom they come into contact. An antique dealer will accumulate scores of visiting cards, and after a week or two they will mean very little. A dealer's name and address in a diary, with a note as to why the name is there (buyer, seller, collector, etc., and of what) can serve a useful purpose.

If the dealer is registered for VAT an Invoice Book is essential. The VAT level was raised to a turnover of £18,000 per year to allow small businesses to operate without registering, but dealers are reminded that this is only £350 a week. There are two systems of VAT applicable to antique dealers. Ordinary VAT is 15 per cent of the total price. Using this system a dealer does not have to prove to whom an article was sold or from whom it was bought. The special scheme is 15 per cent of gross profit. Obviously this is preferable, but to participate in the special scheme the dealer has to have proof of buying—a name and address—and proof of selling—a name, address and invoice.

An added complication is introduced by foreign buyers, who do not need to pay VAT. There are two kinds of form for stamping by customs officials for returning to the seller, one for use by countries in the Common Market and the other for countries outside it. The Common Market form may or may not be stamped by the customs officials of the country of entry, and although officials *should* comply they often refuse simply because it is of no concern to them and merely adds to what they deem to be unnecessary paperwork.

The VAT form relating to goods destined for a country outside the Common Market is stamped by British customs, and returned to the British dealer by the buyer. The British customs officials do their duty, but the onus is on the foreign buyer to comply with the regulations. To make it easier for the foreign buyer, one should have the forms made out as fully as possible and supply a stamped addressed envelope so that all the buyer has to do is to find a post-box.

Alternatively the dealer can charge a foreign buyer VAT and refund it when the forms are received back. It is therefore to the advantage of the buyer to return the forms, but this means that initially he will have to pay more for the goods.

When a dealer is using shippers the shipper will normally supply proof of export for VAT purposes, and this will relieve the dealer of a certain amount of trouble. The important thing is to read the books supplied by Customs and Excise very thoroughly, and to obtain books that deal with antique selling and exporting when VAT is involved. It is in respect of VAT that a good accountant is worth his weight in gold.

It is important to remember that VAT is not entirely one way, and that money is not always flowing in one direction—outwards. On items on which VAT is charged, and which for a 'private' person is so much lost money, VAT can be claimed back. VAT accounts are made up every three months.

For VAT applied to postal exports, there are two basic forms, one to stick on the parcel (VAT form 444), and one to have receipted at the post office when the parcel is posted, to be retained by the sender as proof of dispatch.

VAT is unquestionably time-consuming, and many dealers have refashioned their business to accommodate VAT as conveniently as possible. For a dealer with a big turnover made up of lots of smallish items VAT is obviously more demanding than for a dealer with a similar turnover made up of fewer items, and there is more logic in engaging in a lot of paperwork for expensive items. Exporting expensive antiques will perhaps warrant the use of a shipper, and the consequent increase of essential paperwork, whereas the profit margin from smaller items will not.

A word of warning about foreign buyers. It is to their advantage for a purchase to be over a hundred years old, and foreign dealers will often ask for the invoice to be marked thus, whether, in fact, the articles are over a hundred years old or not. Because of Common Market import dues, it is also to the foreign dealer's advantage for the amount on the invoice to be less than the amount paid. This has become so flagrant that customs officials at the point of entry on the Continent now make their own valuations, ignoring the falsified invoice.

Naturally a dealer wants to make a sale, but most dealers prefer it to be a straight-forward sale without any hanky-panky about fake dates and wrong invoice amounts. If the dealer refuses to go along with the foreigner's wishes the sale may fall through, but in most cases the foreigner will still buy. Antiques of all kinds are still much cheaper in Britain than in the rest of Europe, despite the stronger pound, and fiddling the invoices does not make much difference in the long run, perhaps reducing gross profit by a few per cent. Looked at in another way, it seems impertinent on the part of foreign dealers to assume that British dealers will willingly give false documentation which, whether one likes it or not, is a criminal offence.

The provision of a ledger is optional, and although it is useful where a dealer has a permanent relationship with other dealers, it has no real place in the casual buying and selling cycle. Unlike most other businesses, credit is rarely extended in the antique trade, and a tyro dealer who decided to submit a bill once a month for goods bought would soon be out of business. A ledger is probably necessary for shippers who deal solely with a few large buyers.

A dealer often has a false notion of the profit being made because he fails to take into account the numerous expenses of the trade. It is easy to assume that the difference between buying price and selling price is clear profit, only to wonder where the money has gone. Most dealers prefer to think that they are doing tolerably well (whatever they say to their associates), and there is a tendency to overlook car expenses, telephone calls, extra costs in transporting big furniture, stationery, casual help in the shop, 'back-handers' to auction room porters and other kinds of commission, the cost of tools, polishes, and the thousand-and-one minor items.

An often overlooked expense is the fine that arises from a parking infringement. In the course of business a dealer will often be obliged to park on double yellow lines or in other no-go areas, and in certain towns and cities this can mean an automatic £10 debit. As has been mentioned before, a dealer with good parking facilities outside is to be envied.

Regular payments such as rent and the cost of stalls at markets and fairs are easy to keep track of. To keep an account of money spent on petrol and oil it is convenient to buy these at garages which accept payment by credit card, the monthly statements then provide details of such motor expenses.

If the dealer employs staff it is necessary to keep a wages book. Many dealers deliberately keep their operations on the small side so that they can cope without having to employ an outsider, for not only do wages have to be taken into consideration but NHI contributions and the nuisance of deducting income tax under the PAYE system. It is a lucky dealer indeed who finds it worthwhile to employ help in his shop.

11 Dealing in books and postcards

Many antique dealers find that buying and selling second-hand or antiquarian books offers a profitable side-line, and although bookshelves take up a considerable amount of wall space the advantages far outweigh the disadvantages, the chief of which is the propensity of book buyers to browse and block the shop. Bookshelves should therefore be situated in a part of the shop where there is no congestion, preferably at the back of the shop where the dealer can keep an eye on the browsers. There is a kind of kleptomania associated with books, and the most unlikely people will slip a book into a pocket without paying for it.

A bookseller has more individual items than an antique dealer, but the turnover is usually slower and to compensate for this a bookseller would expect to make a profit of 100 per cent on 'trade' books. A dealer in antiques can undercut the second-hand bookseller because it is a side-line and not survival.

Before the war an antiquarian book dealer would concentrate on leather-bound books, but except for a few select dealers most of them have spread their interests and leather-bound books now represent a minor part of the trade. Leather-bound books should always be bought irrespective of the contents, for they are used by interior decorators as furnishing pieces and old volumes of sermons often find themselves in the most astonishing places.

The first decision an antique dealer has to make if a move into books is contemplated is whether or not to buy and sell anything that comes his way. This approach is not to be recommended. Novels, except for first editions by well known authors, take up an excessive share of space and are slow movers. There will always be buyers of paperbacks at 10p or so, but unless one has a stall in a street market and is selling in quantity paperbacks are more trouble than they are worth. Discretion is also needed when contemplating the purchase of 'collected works'. At the beginning of the century many publishers, often backed by newspaper tycoons, issued cheap editions of the classics, complete with bookcases. In their drab uniform jackets, and with the odd volume missing, they are to be avoided, alongside home encyclopaedias, *Readers' Digest* anthologies and abridgements, and most nineteenth-century theology. There is a popular conception that Victorian Bibles are worth acquiring. These are sometimes very impressive, and are highly valued by private sellers for whom they represent distant antiquity, but there is little or no demand for them despite their often magnificent bindings.

There is a market for all nineteenth-century books dealing with specialized subjects, the more technical the better, and all books prior to 1882 with prints are worth looking at. In 1882 the half-tone process was first used, and consequently photography began to take a primary role in book illustration. The prints in post-1882 books are likely to be half-tone reproductions, and thus of no real interest. Somewhat battered nineteenth-century illustrated books are known as 'breakers'; the prints are removed, and sold separately. Atlases are often split up, and the maps framed and sold at extravagant prices. Victorian books with real photographs stuck on to the pages are highly regarded; the 1970s have seen the prices of old photographs rocketing.

How does a dealer new to the game find out about book prices? The most obvious way is to browse around second-hand bookshops getting the feel of the prices. These will be the retail prices. An accurate guide to the prices the trade is willing to pay can be assessed by subscribing to the weekly trade journal *The Bookdealer* (Sardinia House, Sardinia Square, London WC2) where dealers advertise books they have for sale and for books they want. The old-established *The Clique* is solely used by dealers who want to buy specific books, and is not nearly so helpful. The yearly handbook of the book trade is *Book Prices Current*, but as with all price guides values can be distorted by the conditions under which a certain item was sold. Two or three keen bidders can carry the auction price of a book outside the realm of reason, and the state of a book is of primary importance. If a book has its original dust-jacket it can make the difference between being desirable and uninteresting. Subscribing to a regular book auction room for its catalogues and price lists can be helpful. The most important book auction room is Hodgson's, which is run by Sotheby's. The main snag is that books are often grouped in lots, and there is no way of discovering what an individual book in a lot was worth to the purchaser.

Trends in antiques can be fleeting, a response to an article in a Sunday colour supplement or some bright interior decorator's fad, but trends in books are usually longer lasting and invariably leave some residue. Beautifully produced books will always be worth collecting, as will fine antiques. Although there are some excellent books on book collecting, there are few systematic price guides of the kind that have taken some of the fun out of antiques, and antique dealers who decide to stock books still have an uncluttered field, if they steer clear of classic collectables. The 1960s and early 1970s saw a curious passion of Victorian three-decker novels (novels published in three volumes), and the 1970s have seen the same sort of fervour devoted to highly illustrated books, many of them written for children, dating from the first four decades of the present century. The illustrators include such artists as Rackham, Pogany, and Heath Robinson, the common element of which is a combination of fantasy and meticulous detail.

There is a considerable postal trade in second-hand and antiquarian books, but antique dealers should be warned that postal dealing can be very time consuming, and the high cost of postage does not make it worth while to deal in books priced at less than a pound. It is amazing, too, how much time can be spent merely parcelling books up. On the other hand, if a dealer comes across a book which seems to be valuable it is worthwhile advertising in one of the trade papers, inviting offers. The advertising rates of the book trade papers are ridiculously low, and surely it is worth spending 50p or so to net perhaps £30 or £40, if not more. Of course, one can put a potentially valuable book in a book auction room with a realistic reserve and see how it goes.

Private sellers with books to dispose of often have odd ideas of their value, rating commonplace reference books highly and yet scorning books of real interest. Most value is put on sets of books, simply because they look nice in a bookcase. Even more than when faced with boxes of broken china and tourist vases from Italy a dealer in books has to learn to say 'no' without giving offence, which is not too easy when faced with Harmsworth's *History of the World* in umpteen daunting volumes and widely regarded as a classic by the owner.

Junk shops are not very good places to buy books. They are usually knee-deep in paperbacks and horrendous novels, and the owners get so little decent stuff that they are inclined to overrate it and place ludicrous prices on it. House-calls are by far the best source. With the decline in book-owning, there is now a tendency for books to be regarded as oddities that merely clutter up cupboards.

Somewhat akin to dealing in books is dealing in music. Sheet music is something which one buys in bulk, and with the price of new classical music (the Beethoven sonatas are several pounds a volume) it is worthwhile considering music as a side-line—but only if one has the room. One should be wary of 'popular' music. The 'evergreens' of the 1920s and 1930s have a certain small value, but the great mass of popular music is ephemeral and worthless. If the covers of 1920s and 1930s popular sheet music are 'characteristic' they are worth keeping, bearing in mind that they are due for their turn as collectables.

The most valuable covers are those of Victorian music hall songs, which are colour printed by lithographic methods. These have now been collected for some years and they are not likely to be encountered in dealers' shops or in well-established second-hand bookshops. A dog-eared pile of music will indicate that the contents have been thoroughly researched by sheet-music freaks. In any job lot of music, interesting Victorian covers are remarkably scarce, even in music 'fresh' from a private call-out.

Classical piano music is the most saleable category if the music is considered apart from the decorative covers. Modern music is particularly welcomed by pianists, especially collected works rather than singles, but almost all piano music, even the tame Victorian salon pieces, have a market. Violin and cello music is also in demand, though it is important to ensure that it is complete with the piano part. Songs are very difficult to dispose of, and so is religious music, especially oratorios. Organ music sometimes takes a long time to sell.

The disadvantage of sheet music is that it easily falls apart, and the pages get muddled. In old music the staples have become rusty over the years and have rotted away. A surprising amount of music is Sellotaped, or joined with brown tape, or amateurishly resewn. To make matters worse, this tattered music is often covered with brown paper. A quarter of all music bought in bulk can be instantly disposed of.

One or two book dealers have investigated the possibilities of postal dealing in music, but almost all have found that it does not pay. Even more than in postal book dealing, the cost of postage is prohibitive.

Dealers are always tempted to look for new fields. At first glance, one of the most attractive of the new collectables is the 78 rpm shellac gramophone record, but novice dealers should be warned. There are tons of 78 rpm records about, most of them worthless. They belong to a curious category of lumber; owners hang on to them, thinking that one day they will play them, but the delights of hi-fi and stereophonic sound have wooed them away from the crackle of the old 78 and they do not get played. Eventually they are disposed of. The only sure-fire certainties are jazz and dance-band records, early rag-time, and antediluvian opera singers (and then only some of them). Classical records are almost worthless, with the possible exception of certain favoured piano recordings.

Old gramophone records are heavy, prone to breaking, difficult to store, space-consuming, and attract enthusiasts who are not only space-consuming but time-consuming. This is also true of postcard collectors. Gone are the days when a postcard was something stuck in an album and forgotten. It is now an art-form with a corpus of literature including yearly price guides and periodicals.

Picture postcards have much in common with books. The oddest subjects can command bizarre prices. Among the more collectable categories are cards which deal with sports, especially the Olympic Games of the early 1900s, cards which depict railway stations, post-offices, tram-cars and early buses, any kind of disaster, Suffragettes and Suffragette themes, and anything to do with early aviation. Mildly erotic postcards command several pounds apiece, remarkable when one can buy a complete book of naughty nudes for the same price as one postcard. Comic postcards depend for their value on the artist, as do kiddy cards of the school of Mabel Lucie Attwell.

The most valuable cards are not, as beginners might suppose, the embroidered silk cards of World War I vintage but *art nouveau* cards by artists such as Kirchner and Mucha, with cat postcards by Louis Wain coming up solidly behind. More than most categories of collectables, postcard values have boomed since the mid-1970s, and to keep in touch with rising prices ownership of a postcard price guide is invaluable. Unlike postage stamps, where the market prices bear little relationship to catalogue prices, a postcard dealer sticks by his valuations, usually giving two-thirds of the catalogue value to sellers. Buyers of postcards might find it worthwhile turning the cards over to see if there is anything unusual in the way of postmarks. Postal history is a somewhat esoteric subject, pursued only by those with a taste for it; any postcard with 'pacquet-bot' as a postmark is worth a pound or two (the card was posted on a ship). The stamps on postcards are almost always common and worth nothing.

In general, British postcards are preferable to foreign ones (unless they are very early—the Europeans went into postcards in the nineteenth century and these pioneer cards are much collected); city and town scenes are preferable to country scenes; close-ups of trams, trains, buses, and aircraft are much more desirable than middle-distance scenes or long shots; cathedrals and church pictures are not wanted at all. As collecting postcards was a widespread Edwardian hobby, most postcards were placed in albums. When taken out, the corners often became bent; this can kill the value of a postcard. If an album is bought containing postcards it is better to either sell the lot as a collection or carefully cut the cards out of the album rather than risk damaging the corners.

Slightly off the beaten track but in the same general category as books, postcards, and sheet-music are autographed letters, known as ALSs. LSs are letters signed, only the signature being in the handwriting of the sender; LSs are mostly typewritten letters. DocSs are documents signed. There is amazing money in ALSs: a letter signed by Lenin sold for £680 at auction in 1972. It is a field where there is encouragement to forgers, and a general antique dealer cannot be expected to be an expert in paper, ink, or handwriting. Nineteenth-century publishers had a habit of inserting very good facsimile letters in their books, and these can be convincing. Autograph albums, even when they contain signatures of the famous, are of much less value. The contents of ALSs have a lot of bearing on their worth.

If ALSs are bought among a job lot of books and papers, and it is reasonable to assume that they are genuine and fresh on the market, it is wise to get qualified advice. It is a very specialized subject, little followed outside London, and the average auctioneer, usually so well-versed in everything, is likely to be foxed.

There is a minor market for parchment deeds, and it is difficult for most antique dealers to find out why there is any demand, for they are deadly boring. The late 1970s also saw a curious interest in share certificates, preferably those issued by quaint obsolete companies. These certificates, many of them spectacular and colourful, are framed and stuck up in offices, no doubt providing talking points for those with nothing better to do with their time.

Appendix:
Art and antiques at auction

At the close of 1978 Philips, the auctioneers, asked its specialists what had done well in 1978 and what classes of antiques were worth keeping an eye on in the future. Philips came up strongly behind Sotheby's and Christie's and it is worth noting that many shrewd provincial dealers prefer placing goods into Philips' auction rooms rather than into Sotheby's or Christie's.

	1978 *Items strongest in demand or price appreciation*	1979 *Items worth watching*
Furniture	Sets of chairs; oak of all periods; Edwardian and Victorian, including reproduction; Decorative Continental; Dutch marquetry.	Eighteenth-century mahogany and all good period English; progressive furniture from 1900 onwards.
Paintings, watercolours, prints	Quality Victorian paintings, academic and decorative; Dutch marines; English nineteenth- and twentieth-century landscapes. Watercolours—signed and dated early English, good Victorian and Dutch nineteenth century; good period sporting, topographical and Old Master prints.	English nineteenth-century paintings; quality English watercolours; mezzotints; modern British prints.

Objets d'art clocks, watches, etc.	Good bronzes, especially nineteenth-century French; statuary of all types; chandeliers; scientific instruments.	Marble statuary; good early nineteenth-century clocks; pewter and metalware.
Ceramics and glass	Coloured Worcester; Delft, slipware; Wedgwood; eighteenth-century figures; French paperweights; Mason's ironstone; Continental enamel boxes; finely engraved glasses.	Twentieth-century Royal Worcester figures and animals; eighteenth-century figures; eighteenth-century drinking glasses; fine cameo glass; nineteenth-century engraved glass.
Silver, gold, and plate	George III candlesticks; small Georgian; late Victorian/Edwardian small silver; eighteenth-century French, Dutch, German; electroplate, especially Victorian.	Silver and gold boxes, matchcases, etc.; electroplate.
Books and ephemera	Books with topographical views (e.g. early Germany); natural history with colour plates; maps of America, Australasia; military documents.	Sporting subject books; nineteenth- and twentieth-century photographs; film posters.

On more general lines, Phillips' specialists speculated that any antique small enough to be carried in the hand was likely to rise in value, and picked out coins, gold and silver boxes, netsukes, watches, small silver, and jewellery. Sotheby's confirmed this trend, selecting snuff-boxes, carved ivories, pendants and antique jewellery as extra-desirable.

Collectors' items likely to rise in price were, according to both Sotheby's and Phillips, quality toys. Locomotives and steam-powered items rose dramatically during 1978. The toys of the 1940s have their collectors. Phillips' experts also note the sudden interest in chandeliers; two years ago auction rooms were turning them away. There is also a somewhat surprising enthusiasm for marble statuary.

If one looks at the list there is nothing startling, except perhaps the mention of 'progressive' furniture. This would seem to mean experimental and modernistic furniture, anticipated in the late nineteenth century by Rennie Mackintosh and served up in later years as G-plan. Dealers will hope that the promise held out for mezzotints is fulfilled, as they have folders full of them. Nothing too much should be expected of the modern prints that every shop has in abundance, though fakers will be pleased by their inclusion as they will no doubt trust that the current steady trade in modern 'original' signed prints will improve.

High quality chandeliers with hundreds of cut-glass drops have, contrary to Phillips' view, never been out of fashion. Rather the reverse. They belong to a class of antique which, if realistically priced, is immediately snapped up by the private buyer without the necessity of placing it in auction. Marble statuary has been brought to light because it is now worth a dealer's while handling it. It belongs to a category which the average dealer would prefer to stay clear of—the enormous mirror group. Immensely heavy and needing more sophisticated lifting gear than three or four brawny humpers, marble statuary tends to stay where it is unless big money is involved. However, the interest is not new. In the 1960s when all antiques were relatively cheap the most famous Victorian marble statue, John Gibson's 'The Tinted Venus', made several thousand pounds at Sotheby's, Belgravia.

Index